DIY Tel Aviv

The alternative City Guide

2014 Edition

Cover art by: Yotam Fiszbein (yotamfi@gmail.com)
If you like it as much as I do – give him some work!

Proudly self published – Support global DIY culture by buying from independent publishers

Visit the DIY Tel Aviv website:
www.diytelavivguide.com

Contents

INTRO **11**

    Support this guide 12

    A note for students... 13

1 Useful stuff **14**

    Getting in and out of Tel Aviv 15

    Getting More info 16

        Tel Aviv official tourist information 16

  Issues... 17

  The Jewish thing 17

        Kosher 17

        Shabat 18

        Will I get blown up? 19

        Religious and national holidays 19

        Tel Aviv festivals & big events 25

        Internet 26

        Phones 29

Money 30

Crime 32

Emergencies 32

Chemists / Pharmacies 33

Medical Care / Doctors 34

Laundry 35

Women's Issues 36

LGBT 38

Sex 40

Alcohol 42

Cigarettes and the smoking ban 43

Drugs 44

2 Sleep **46**

Hotels 47

Hostels 48

Self-catering holiday flats 50

Sublets 52

Stay with locals 54

3 Get around **58**

Cycling 58

Roller blades / skateboards 66

Cars 66

Motorbikes and mopeds 68

Segways..69

Taxis..69

Buses...70

Shared Taxis (moniyot sheirut)...........................73

Trains...74

Walking..74

4 Buy food. Eat food. **75**

Supermarkets..75

Markets..76

Health food stores..79

Street food / Fast food 81

Falafel, Hummus and Sabich...............................84

Burekas..86

5

Pizza 88

Asian 89

Health Food/ veggie / vegan 90

Malawah and Jahnun 91

Bakeries, patisseries, sandwiches 92

Coffee, tea, spices and sweets 96

Alcohol 98

Ice cream 99

Juice Bars 101

5 Eat Out. Drink Out **103**

Restaurants 104

Hot Spots 104

Cheap and cheerful local flavours 109

Italian 112

Spanish / tapas 114

Asian 115

Vegetarian / Vegan 119

Various Jewish home-cooked meals 121

Mexican...122

African..123

Bars and dance bars...125

Israeli Drinking habits.......................................125

Dance Bars...126

Bars with live music (almost) every night...............129

Mingling, hanging out..130

Bars with good food..136

Other bars..138

Cafés..140

On the menu..140

Laptop-friendly cafés..141

Other Cafés...144

6 Buy stuff 148

Shopping Centres..148

Markets...149

Clothes / shoes / accessories...........................151

Areas..151

Club / Cyber / Goth / Hippie / Street Clothes.........154

Vintage and retro clothes...156

Designer Clothing and accessories..........................160

Hair and body..164

Books..166

Art & Design..170

Music..171

Misc...172

Online Shopping..173

General...173

Art, design and related stuff.....................................174

Fashion and accessories..175

7 Do Stuff...176

Hang out...176

Tours, workshops, lectures.......................................178

Yoga and meditation..183

Exercise, swimming and pilates.............................185

Dancing...187

Juggling / circus / drumming/ Jamming 189

Water sports 190

Cinema 191

8 Art & Stuff **193**

Spaces 193

Street Art 197

9 Party. Club. Gig. **199**

Going out in Tel Aviv 199

Finding out what's happening 200

Clubs and venues 203

Check out the talent 209

10 Volunteering, Activism, Politics **214**

Activism centres & locations 214

Volunteering, internships, opportunities 216

General Humanitarian Causes 216

Health 218

Feminist/ women 218

LGBT 220

Refugees & migrant workers................................220

Political activism & study tours 221

More peace organisations offering opportunities...225

Animals, farming, environment.........................227

More Information 229

11 Out of town festivals 232

Out of town parties...234

10

INTRO

Welcome to the 4th edition of DIY Tel Aviv!

For the past 4 years DIY Tel Aviv has been connecting people like you with the coolest things this city has to offer. This edition is the best so far, so dig in!

I've written this guide to answer the sort of questions I always ask when I travel, things like: 'Where's the party?'; 'Where do the cool kids here go?'; 'Where can I find a good yoga class?'; 'Where can I get booze/ pizza / cake at two in the morning?'...You know the sort of stuff. This is why you'll find a lot of random stuff in this guide, alongside normal stuff like accommodation, transport, basic tourist info, etc.. Tel Aviv is certainly random, which is what makes it great, as far as I'm concerned.

Travel for me is about all those little surreal and magical moments that make every long journey worthwhile. I hope this guide will help you find some of your own magical moments during your stay in Tel Aviv, or at the very least point you in the direction of places that don't suck.

Enjoy your trip!

Shimrit, Tel Aviv

Support this guide

If you've enjoyed this guide, please help spread the word so that others may enjoy it:

- Tell people about it (Facebook, Twitter, face to face)

- Review it on Amazon (It really helps!)

- If you haven't already: pay for the guide. Writing this guide is a full time job and I need the money I make from selling it so I can pay my rent. If you didn't pay for this guide but have used it and enjoyed it, my Paypal email address is info@diytelavivguide.com. You can use it to send me money. Thanks!

A very very special thanks to my helpers, advisors, tippers and supporters: Yotam (who did the cover), Vicki, Tal, Noa & Daniel, Kutner, Ilana, Tair, Shiri, Gili Pliskin, Johannes Päch, Colin Bulka, David Jarkowski, Blake Zelickson

One more thing...

This guide is always in flux – I am a borderline dyslexic with zero design skills and poor attention to detail. I often work on the guide when I come home from clubbing and am drunk and tired. To make things worse, underground culture shifts and changes frequently and Tel Aviv is constantly renewing. If you find anything in this guide inaccurate, email me at: **info@diytelavivguide.com**. DIY Tel Aviv is also on Twitter (**@diytelaviv**), Google Places (http://bit.ly/irjrTQ) and Facebook (**http://www.facebook.com/diytelaviv**)

A note for students...

When I wrote this guide, I was thinking of you too, not just tourists. If you're going to be studying in an exciting city like Tel Aviv, you may as well get a head start on finding scenes to belong to, places to go and practical things like cheap bike shops, etc. However, you'll note that there aren't really many interesting things listed in the Ramat Aviv area, where the University is. This is because, generally speaking, the only interesting things in Ramat Aviv are the things directly to do with the University itself. It's a fairly suburban area without much in the way of nightlife and excitement. If you're interested in city life outside of Uni, your best bet is to find somewhere to live that's south of the Yarkon river. Even the cheaper, more happening southern neighbourhoods are well connected to the Uni by means of bus and train. It's easier to catch a bus or a train to and from the Uni in the day than it is to get home to Ramat Aviv at 4AM after a night of heavy drinking in town. The accommodation section of this guide will tell you where to look rooms and flats.

Of course, you might be living in the dorms, in which case, head down to the commercial centre at Brodetsky 17, where you will find the area's student bar (**Rosh Pina** * 03 – 6427062 * 19:00 – last customer) and a good café / bistro frequented by students (**Beta Caffé** *   http://bit.ly/ITf8oS * 03 – 6412285 * Sun – Sat 8:00 – 00:00). Next door is one of the Bigudyot (see Buy Stuff / Clothes / Vintage) where you can supposedly get really good deals on secondhand designer (and other) clothes.
You might also want to check out **Abu Shay** at http://goo.gl/nEMTh (Facebook page) or at abu.shay2013@gmail.com. It's a home food delivery service set up especially for stuents. It's cheap and tasty and great for those exam periods when you can't get around to cooking or leaving the house! Meat / veggie / vegan dishes available.

1 Useful stuff

This guide comes with a Google Map. It lives at:

http://tinyurl.com/3yfsgzz

Most of the places listed in this guide are marked on the map and colour coded according to their type.

Note that street and place names in Tel Aviv are a bit of a point of contention. They are often written phonetically and everyone has a different version of spelling them in English. You'll sometimes see several different spellings on the same street – on road signs, shop signs, etc.

Google Maps mostly follow the official spelling, which is often not the one that's commonly used by people. I've mostly gone with Google's version, but I do point out some obvious cases when the "proper" version differs from the version usually in use.

You can get real maps at hotels, souvenir shops, Stiematzky shops (see Shopping section / books) and the tourist info places below. Free (crap) tourist maps are also available around town. Try AM:PM stores (see Food section / supermarkets). The more basic maps will sometimes not have the Southern areas like Florentin on them, so you might want to print out or familiarise yourself with the Google map I made. At the end of this guide are a few maps I got off OpenStreetMap using a free bit of software called Maperitive. They should be useful as a reference for when you don't have access to the Internet and a proper map. Using free software and services helps keep the price of this guide low and, let's face it, most guidebook maps are pretty shit. At least these are accurate.

There is an online version of this guide that updates more or less once a month. An official new edition comes out around April each year. The online version of the guide costs £5 for unlimited downloads of the current edition's updates. You can get it from www.diytelavivguide.com.

Getting in and out of Tel Aviv

Israeli immigration controls and security at the airport can be notoriously tough in both directions. You should arrive at Ben Gurion airport at least 3 hours before the scheduled departure when leaving the country, as clearing security and immigration can take a long time. If you're flying into Israel with an Israeli airline, you'll need to also arrive at your departure airport 3 hours before your flight as the airline will have its own extra security checks for you to clear.

Some people seem to have no trouble getting in and out of Israel, while others get heaps of hassle. If you are (or look like) a Muslim, a migrant worker, a hippie or a foreign peace activist, it's best to mentally prepare yourself for lots of annoying questions and bag searches. This way, you can be pleasantly surprised if things go smoothly (which they sometimes do), rather than unpleasantly surprised if your security or immigration person happens to be a dick (which they sometimes are) or extra thorough (which they often are).

From the airport you can either take a train or a private ("special") taxi to get into Tel Aviv. The train takes about 15 minutes to get into town and is relatively cheap. For an easy life, get off at the Central (Savidor) station where there are signs in English and it's easier to get a bus or a taxi to other parts of town (but see the Getting Around Tel Aviv section for taxi info first).

Other stations may be closer to where you're going but may be more difficult to find your way from when you've just landed.

While the train does run all night, which is cool, it doesn't run on Shabat (see below), which is crap. While there are always shared taxis going to Jerusalem from the airport, there aren't any to Tel Aviv. It means your only option for getting to or from the airport when the train isn't running (Friday afternoon till late Saturday evening) is to take an expensive private taxi or hire a car. A taxi to Tel Aviv costs around 140NIS. To get from town to the airport, try **Hadar Taxis** (03-9711103) first, which may be cheaper (they're based near the airport itself and need to get their taxis back there from town).

When taking a taxi from the airport, always and I mean always go to the designated taxi point where registered taxis line up. Women especially should beware of getting into unofficial, unregistered taxis.

Getting More info

Tel Aviv official tourist information

They provide friendly advice, free maps and information about everything from hotels to tours and restaurants. Obviously not alternative but sometimes useful.

Tayelet office (Tel Aviv Promenade / seafront)
Herbert Samuel 46 (corner of Geula 2) * 03-5166188
Sun - Thurs, 09:30 -17:30, Fri, 09:30- 13:00

City Hall Lobby
Ibn Gavirol 69 * 03- 521-8500
Open: Sunday - Thursday, 09:00 until 14:00

For unofficial info check out Facebook group **Secret Tel Aviv**. It has evolved into a place where people ask and give advice (mostly in English) about all aspects of living in Tel Aviv / Israel. You can also find stuff for sale, places to live and all kinds of odd requests fulfilled there.

Issues...

Israel has a few interesting "quirks", shall we say. Here are some things that are worth knowing about the way things work here.

The Jewish thing

Kosher

The vast majority of the food places and shops in Tel Aviv are Kosher. Without going too far into the whole thing, what it means to you (unless you keep Kosher) is that Kosher places won't serve both dairy and meat products (it's either one or the other) and will have some restrictions when serving meat and fish. A meat restaurant won't even serve you real milk with the coffee, while a Kosher pizza place will serve fish but not meat.

Properly Kosher places are also not open on the Shabat (see below) and don't serve leavened products during Passover (see below). Many of the restaurants in this guide are not Kosher.

Shabat

The Jewish day of rest is somewhat of a big deal and is, of course, the Saturday (Shabat). The Shabat "enters" at sunset on Friday evening and "exits" at sunset on Saturday evening.

Israel now operates a 5 day week, the extra free day being Friday (as that was only ever a half day anyway). Friday afternoon involves lots of rushing around, as people get ready for Shabat, or lots of sitting around in cafés, going to Jaffa for hummus or sleeping off Thursday night's hangover.

Most stores close early on Friday and are closed on the Saturday, even if not otherwise Kosher. Having a customary day of rest protected by law and religion is not a custom people are keen to give up.

Saturday itself often feels very sleepy and peaceful – sort of like how a Sunday feels in a small Catholic village – which is quite funny considering how busy and buzzy Tel Aviv is normally. There's no public transport till Saturday evening (apart from taxis and some shared taxis) and most stores are shut, though nowadays there are plenty of newsagents and mini-markets that stay open. Most cafés and restaurants, those that are not Kosher, that is, stay open and get very busy. Some close to give the owners a rest.

Will I get blown up?

Tel Aviv is the safest place in Israel in terms of both terrorist activity and aerial bombardments. Even with the recent fighting, it was quickly protected and damage was minimal. Here's hoping the ceasefire holds. Meanwhile, you'll still see signs of the conflict around anyway. You will see a lot of soldiers around (not on guard, usually, just walking about on their way somewhere else) and you'll have your bags searched going into most big public buildings, generally by rather indifferent security guards. Remember these guys are doing a fairly dangerous job for minimum wage, so please be nice to them. They really don't give a shit about what's in your bag, unless it's a weapon or a bomb. The security guy on the door is always the first to go in case of a real suicide bomber attack, usually saving a lot of people in the process.

Israelis are incredibly twitchy about suspect packages, so don't leave your luggage unattended even for a minute unless you want to see it blown up by a police robot. If you spot something suspicious yourself, grab a local and let them know immediately, people here are taught the correct procedure from age 0 and no one would hold it against you if you're over cautious.

Religious and national holidays

Israel's official calendar is the Jewish calendar, which is a lunar calendar. All the Jewish holidays, plus the official non-religious festivals are set according to this calendar. While some holidays are fun, some may pose weird and interesting problems, so if you're planning a holiday, check out the information below before committing to any dates.

Like the Shabat, Israeli holidays start and finish on a sunset.

For an exact calendar of the Jewish holidays and a proper explanation of what they're all about see: http://www.chabad.org/holidays/default_cdo/jewish/Holidays.htm

For this guide, I've chosen to concentrate on what these holidays mean to you in real terms as a non-Jewish tourist.

Rosh Hashana (Usually around September)

A religious holiday – the Jewish New Year. Involves 2 days of Shabat-like rest and big meals with the family. Everything shuts.

Yom Kippur (10 days after Rosh Hashana)

The holiest day in the Jewish calendar. Everything, and I mean everything is shut, save for places in deepest darkest Jaffa. Religious and even most (supposedly) secular Israelis fast from the evening before the holiday and the more devout ones visit the synagogue. All Israeli TV channels are off as are all radio stations, apart from a single station on the military network that plays sad Israeli songs all day long. Apart from the occasional ambulance, you won't see any cars on the road either. Non-religious Israelis and their kids jump on their bicycles en mass and head to the motorways, enjoying the car-free day.

Sukkot (a few days following Yom Kippur)

Involves two days of Shabat-like rest, with the rest of the week being a semi-holiday where official things like government offices and the post offices operate reduced opening hours. There are often festivals during this time, including Israel's fringe theatre festival in Acco.

Hanukah (usually around December)

The Jewish answer to Christmas is somewhat of a more muted affair in Israel, where there's no competition for the affection of the kids.

Candles are lit nightly for 8 days and there are often plenty of cool events in town, though mostly for kids. Israeli kids don't get the multitude of presents their European and American counterparts get, but they do get chocolate coins and plenty of fried food including my favourite food – doughnuts! Head over to **Roladin** café at Ibn Gabirol 24 for the best selection. They set up a special stall by the café and come up with new and exciting varieties every year.

Purim (usually around March)

The Jewish Halloween. It's not about fending off the evil spirits, but rather the celebration of luck, fate and triumph over adversity. Tel Aviv turns into one giant costume party with events starting days before the holiday and culminating in both organised and impromptu parties all over.

According to tradition, you are expected to get drunk to the point of "Ad Lo Yada", which translates loosely into being so drunk you no longer know who and where you are.

The people of Tel Aviv take this custom very seriously, as do their neighbours who flock to the city to party in its streets. Keep your ears open for the exact date of the massive street parties that happen every year in Florentin, the Jaffa flea market area, Neve Tsedek or Rotschild Blvd. Usually on the closest weekend to the actual holiday.

For cheap costumes, head down to the Levinsky Market area (namely Matalon St. and Herzl between Levinsky and Matalon). The nearby Kfar Giladi St. is also flush with shops selling everything from costumes to make up. These are officially wholesale places, but they often sell to the public too, especially at Purim. If you're feeling creative, Nahalat Binyamin St. is the city's main fabric and haberdashery area. Some fabric shops cash in on the holiday and offer simple costumes too. Shops are scattered both on and off the pedestrianised area and get very busy before the holiday.

If you like cake, check out the holiday's official dish, Oznei Haman (hamentashen), sort of deep filled cookies. The traditional filling is poppy seed, though nowadays you can get anything from chocolate to dulce de leche.

Pesach / Passover (usually around April)

The Jewish spring holiday, sometimes coinciding with Easter. Two days of Shabat-like rest, separated by a week without any decent food, unless you enjoy matza bread and related products. No pizza, no bread, no pita bread, no cakes (apart from some unpleasant "Passover-Kosher" varieties) and almost no booze are Kosher. While many places nowadays defy the holiday and sell their wares as usual, many still don't.

Unless you're a religious Jew who celebrates this holiday by choice, you'll quickly tire of the reduced food and drink options.

Many places in Tel Aviv shut down during Passover as the pressure is increasingly on not to sell leavened products in Jewish public places. Some bars and cafés remain open and serve normal food, so if a non-Kosher place is still open, chances are you'll find something there.

Head for the Tiv Taam shops as well as Jaffa's many Arab bakeries and restaurants if you want to buy bread. Most of Tel Aviv's secular residents end up there sooner or later. There are also some other non Kosher minimarkets in town that have been increasingly selling non-Kosher food, but you never know what laws the government will pass next to stop them. It's a constant struggle.

That aside, the usually fine weather and the holiday can only mean one thing – festivals!

Holocaust Day (generally in April)

The Israeli Holocaust Memorial Day is on a different date than the international one. In keeping with the seriousness of the day, everything becomes a little bit more glum and muted. The day starts with 2 minutes of silence, marked by a special siren (a monotone, rather than the up and down air raid siren). People drop everything and stand silently at attention for 2 minutes. Drivers stop their cars in the middle of the road, get out and stand. Out of respect for the day, it's best if you follow suit. Many Israelis have lost relatives in the Holocaust and get very angry when people appear to disrespect the occasion.

War Memorial Day (Usually around April or May)

The day before Independence Day is marked as war memorial day, with ceremonies all over the country. The beginning of the day is marked on the previous evening by a minute long siren sound. At 11:00 on the day itself there is another siren to mark the beginning of the national ceremonies. Similarly to Holocaust day, people stand at attention out of respect for the fallen. God help you if you're in a public place and don't stand along with them.

The end of the Memorial Day (the evening) marks the beginning of Independence Day and this is when the mad parties start. There have been many debates throughout the years about whether these days should be moved further apart, but in Israel freedom comes with a bloody price tag and no one is ever going to let you forget that.

Independence Day

Following on from War Memorial Day when Tel Aviv once more turns into a giant party with fireworks, celebrations and parties. Traditionally, Florentin turns into a giant street party once more (police permitting), but the atmosphere is usually quite intense and generally viewed as disconnected from the general neighbourhood vibe and style. Still, there's always a good party to go to somewhere in town on the night or the day itself.

Israel's Independence Day is marked by the Palestinian Arabs as the "Nakba day" to commemorate the killing and dislocation of 700,000 Palestinians from their home during the Independence War in 1948 and the creation of the Palestinian refugee problem (the official Nakba Day is May 15).

In 2009, a law was suggested to outlaw the public commemoration of this day, aimed mostly at Israeli Arabs. For this reason, Independence Day is a very controversial day among the Israeli left wing.

Shavuot (May or June)

A couple of days of Shabat-like rest. This is the dairy holiday and harvest holiday, so great for vegetarians, as everywhere is full of delicious veggie dairy food.

Tel Aviv festivals & big events

The dates for these change slightly every year. Check out the websites when possible or look out for posters around town (or check the DIY Tel Aviv blog, obviously).

Tel Aviv Jazz Festival (around February)
www.jazzfest.co.il

A long running and highly popular festival featuring both local and international artists. May not be running annually anymore.

Tel Aviv Marathon (March)
http://www.tlvmarathon.co.il/

The weather is perfect for it and you run by the beach.

Houses from inside / open houses (usually in May)
http://www.batim-il.org/

An urban architecture and interior design event inviting people to take a closer look at urban spaces that are normally closed to the public.

Fresh Paint Art Fair (May)
http://www.freshpaint.co.il/

A big, multi-disciplinary art event with interesting stuff. Usually accompanied by the interesting "rejection salon" for those artists who didn't quite make it.

DocAviv (May)
http://www.docaviv.co.il/

Tel Aviv's brilliant documentary film festival with lots to see, much of which is at the very least subtitled into English.

White Night (usually at the end of June)

The city goes even more 24 hours than usual, with all kinds of exciting late night happenings all over the cities, from museums & galleries opening late to live music, movies, shopping, parties, food and other cool random things.

Animix (August)
http://www.animixfest.co.il

The festival of comics and animation at the Cinemateque. There are usually some very interesting international guests and many films and workshops are in English.

Spirit – spiritual film festival (sometime in autumn)
http://spiritfestival.co.il/

3 days of spiritually inspiring films (hippie stuff and beyond).

Internet

If you have your own laptop or Internet phone then you'll find Tel Aviv the perfect place for getting online any time, any place. Practically every café has a wireless network for public use and even some bars and restaurants have them. In fact, I've even heard that some bad people have discovered that you can actually sit on a bench on any number of streets and boulevards and just find a random unsecured network to use. Of course, unauthorised use of wireless networks is illegal in Israel, so I would never advise you to do that.

If you don't have your own device, your options are a bit more limited. Most hostels offer Internet PCs for use by their guests, plus the big seafront hotels have paid Internet services too. Some self catering apartments also come equipped with computers or laptops (though sometimes for an extra fee). There are also a few Internet cafés around in the main tourist areas (Ben Yehuda St., Dizengoff St. and HaYarkon St.) as well as around the central bus station area, where the majority of Israel's foreign worker and refugee population lives. Prices are generally high in the tourist areas – around 20 NIS per hour, though sometimes that includes a drink. In the central bus station area they can be a lot cheaper – just get on Levinsky St. and you'll find one opposite the garden / park, heading west from the station towards Florentin.

Dizi

Ben Ami 13 (Dizengoff Square by the antiques market and opp the cinema building)
03-522455 * Sun – Sat 8:00 – 24:00 (ish)

This bright, peaceful café doubles as a launderette and a DVD library, so has an obvious appeal for students, making for a young, fun vibe. It rents out laptops for 15-20NIS an hour, so you can feel more like a local while you check your mail.

Log In

Ben Yehuda 21 * 24 hours

A pleasant enough take on the Internet café concept. You can actually order food and drink here, rather than just check your mail.

Interfun

Allenby 20 * 03-5167776 * 10:00 – 4:00

A big, popular Internet Café of the more standard type – less of the café and more of the Internet.

Misantrope

http://misantrope.com (Hebrew only)

Frishman 43 * 074-7031805 * Sun – Thurs 8:30 – 22:00, Fri 10:00 – 22:00, Sat 12:00 – 22:00 (opening hours are often longer, especially during exam periods at local universities)

A guilt free café style workspace (but not a café) where no waiters will bug you while you work. This revolutionary "urban workspace" is a bright space where you pay a low price per hour or per day (max 55NIS per day) and can bring your laptop, work, print and even fax if you need to. You also get free coffee and tea plus cookies and snacks and can buy fresh sandwiches from vending machines at a very low price. There is a covered balcony for talking and meetings.

Heder Avoda (Work room)

King George 105 * 053-7208885/6 * Sun – Thur 9:00 – 22:00, Fri 9:00 – 17:00

Similar to the above, 59NIS per day (or 15NIS for the first hour and 10NIS for each additional hour) buys you a space at this friendly and peaceful communal workspace with a free buffet, 2nd hand books for sale (and a library), plus fax and printing services.

Phones

Israel's dial code is +972 and Tel Aviv's is 03 from within Israel. Drop the 0 if calling from outside. Mobile phone numbers start with 05.

You can buy cheap international calling cards from machines at the airport and from Pitsutsiyot (newsagents) in town. The central bus station area is particularly good for those, because of the big foreign worker population. You can use some of them at the few payphones that remain in town, while others are the sort that would work from any phone, but you need to dial a special number to get patched through.

There are a few mobile phone companies active in Israel. The big ones are Cellcom, Pelephone and Orange, who do pay as you go. There are stalls at the airport that rent out mobile phones but the prices are pretty extortionate. If you think you might need a local phone while you're in Tel Aviv, your best bet is to come equipped with your own unlocked mobile phone and buy a local pay as you go sim. Dual, tri and quad band phones will all work with an Israeli sim. Currently, Orange offer the cheapest deals on sims - you can buy an "Orange Big Talk" sim for around 60NIS including 10NIS of credit. There are Orange stalls in Dizengoff Center, building A and at the central bus station, plus a few more around town. You could also get sims from newsagents where you can also get competing companies' sims, plus recharge your pay as you go phone balance.

Charging is done either by use of a scratch card or automatically by text message: pay at the till, supply your mobile number and receive a text message saying it's been done. Note that the automatic charge network doesn't work on weekends, so either charge before Shabat or buy a scratch card. The charging menu system is in Hebrew if done by scratch card. To change the language of the menu, pick option 7.

PAYG rates are pretty high. However, you don't get charged for incoming calls or text messages and some scratch cards offer some good free minute deals (usually but not always to phones on the same network). Every newsagent will have slightly different ones, often called "big bonus" (on the Orange network at least). You can use some big bonus charge cards for mobile Internet. If you have a smartphone you want to use, buy your sim from an Orange store and let them know what you want to do. They'll be able to advise you further.

It's important to note that there are now some cheaper mobile companies in Israel, namely Hot Mobile and Golan Telecom. If you're going to be in Israel for a while, it may be worth investigating getting a contract with them (minimum is one month). Golan Telecom will let you pay with a foreign credit card and occasionally have deals where you can sign up and get a few months free. If you cancel within that period, you don't pay a dime. Worth checking out.

Money

It's easy enough to exchange money at the Post Office, in banks and at various change points around town. Personally, I get mine out of the wall with my British cards.

Some local banks' cash points are funny with some foreign cards and won't let you have money. Your best bet is to try Bank Leumi and Bank Hapoalim cash points as those generally work best.

English menus are available at all cash points, so you won't have to guess.

During Christmas (and possibly other big Christian holidays when banks abroad are shut) there are sometimes problems accessing the international network, which might mean you won't be able to get money out at all. Best to stock up in advance to be on the safe side. If you get stuck during these times, you'll still be able to use a debit card or credit card in shops.

The Post Office (http://www.israelpost.co.il) now sells a single use pre-charged local Visa card which you can pre-charge with anything from 250 – 1000 NIS and use as you would a normal credit card. It can be handy for some things, especially if you don't like carrying a lot of cash on you. Keep in mind that you can't use it to pay for hotels, car rental, gas / petrol, etc. as well as DVDs rented from vending machines.

The post office bank also offers bank accounts for non-Israeli citizens and its services are the cheapest in the country. I believe you may need an Israeli address but ask for more details at bigger post office branches.

How much???

Tel Aviv is generally no longer a cheap place to visit. Most of your money will go on accommodation and eating / drinking out. Taxi rides, while individually quite cheap, can also add up.

If you're intent on saving money – cycle or walk rather than use public transport, live on cheap, healthy street food rather than posh restaurant food and make full use of happy hours and lunchtime "business deals" to dine out in style. The good news is that underground parties generally have friendlier bar prices, as well as lower ticket prices.

Self-catering will save you lots of money, especially if there are a few of you. Fresh produce and cooking ingredients are relatively cheap in Tel Aviv and holiday flats are often much cheaper than hotel rooms.

Crime

Tel Aviv is fairly safe, but theft and other such nasty petty crimes are pretty common. Outright muggings are not, but that doesn't mean you should venture into dark alleys waving huge wads of cash. In all cases, common sense is your friend – don't leave your stuff unattended in cafés and shops, pay special attention in busy areas and markets, etc.

If something does get stolen, you'll find the local police useless but usually well-meaning. You'll need to go to the police station, report the crime and get a printout to give to your insurance company. If you report a crime at the location (for example, in the case a break in) and are given a handwritten form, you'll still need to go to the station for the print out, though some policemen may mistakenly tell you otherwise.

Sex crime, even if normally "mild", is pretty common in Tel Aviv, sadly. See the Women section below.

Emergencies

Israel's emergency numbers are:

Police: 100

Magen David Adom (ambulance): 101

Fire brigade: 102

Rape / Sexual assault helpline (not the police): 1202

Tel Aviv's council hotline for things like noise pollution, burst pipes on the street, etc. is: **106**

Chemists / Pharmacies

Most chemists operate normal opening hours, usually closing around 19:00 or 20:00. Tel Aviv operates a rotating schedule of 24 / 7 chemists. The schedule is posted on the city's website (http://www.tel-aviv.gov.il/Hebrew/Human/PublicHealth/Pharmacies.asp) every month, but unfortunately it's in Hebrew. There are, however, a few places that are always open 24 hours a day.

24 hour chemists on weekdays:

Superpharm London Ministore
Shaul haMelech 4 (corner of Ibn Gabirol) * Weekdays from Sat 20:00 – Fri 16:00

Superpharm Shikun Dan
Pinhas Rozen 42 (too far north for most people) * 24 hours all week

There is another place on Dizengoff Square that's open till 2:00 in the morning daily.

Chemists open on Shabat:

Superpharm Azrieli
Azrieli Center * Sat 11:00 – 20:00

Superpharm Gordon / Dizengoff
Dizengoff 129 (corner of Gordon) * Sat 8:00 – 20:00

Superpharm Ramat Aviv gimel
Ahimeir 1 * Sat 8:00 – 20:00

Superpharm Jaffa
Sderot Yerushalayim 49 * Sat 8:00 – 20:00

Superpharm Allenby
Allenby 115 (just up from the corner with Yehuda Halevi) * Sat 8:00 – 20:00

Medical Care / Doctors

If you need medical help for anything that doesn't involve an emergency but requires a doctor to look at you and give you a prescription / inject you with something / bandage you up, etc., you can try Bikurofe, a private clinic network. At the time of writing, seeing a doctor there costs 450NIS and is pretty straightforward – you just turn up, register, pay your fee and await your turn. You get a receipt in the end which you can show your insurance company. They have a branch on HaArbaa 20 (03-2642371 * Sun, Tues, Thurs, 19:00 – 1:00, Mon & Wed 16:00 – 1:00, Fri 13:00 – 1:00, Sat 9:00 – 1:00) and another branch on Yigal Alon 90 (03-6272350) which you can contact over night till 6:30AM when the other place is shut.

Physicians for Human Rights (see Politics & Activism section) operate an open clinic in Jaffa for people who are not entitled to and can't afford to be treated anywhere else. If that includes you, look it up. I'm not putting any more details here because you should only use this option if you have no other choice. The clinic is struggling enough as it is so you shouldn't go there if you just want to save a bit of cash.

If your problem is sexual health related, try the **Levinsky Clinic** in the Sex section below.

Laundry

There are self service launderettes all over the city and most are open 24 hours. If you want to have a coffee while you wait, try **Dizi** (above in the Internet section), though it's not open 24 hours. Here's a random selection of self-service locations:

Kikar Dizengoff (Dizengoff Sq.) 6 * Ben Yehuda 102 * Frishman 88 * Ibn Gabirol 109, 59 and 15 (my personal favourite with free wifi, snacks, coffee and even a massage chair). * Sderot Yerushalaim 38, Jaffa * Florentin – Corner of Frenkel & Vital, corner of Florentin & Hakishon *

There are plenty more of those all over, but not all are self service. Prices for serviced laundry vary and if you're washing a lot of clothes, may actually be quite competitive. Machines will often take only 1NIS and 5NIS coins, so get those ready. Wash & dry will often cost 15NIS and up.

Women's Issues

In general, Tel Aviv is very safe for women traveling solo. There are some areas in southern Jaffa (not covered in the guide) that are very Muslim, where it's supposedly not customary for women to be out on their own after dark. Even there you'd only get stared at as far as I know and wouldn't be in any actual danger. In Tel Aviv itself and the mixed parts of Jaffa there are no such restrictions and you can pretty much wear and do what you want.

Be aware, though, that sex crime does happen and tourists / foreigners are often seen as an easy target, so keep your wits about you. Israelis are very friendly, yes, but single men (young and old) who appear friendly to you as a single woman will usually have some sort of hidden agenda. If a man invites you to his house when you've only just met, for example, don't assume it's the famous Israeli hospitality that's behind the gesture. More often than not, the guy will be looking for sex and he may well assume that you want the same if you accept the invitation.

Tel Aviv is not a place where you are expected to cover up, though obviously you'll get more attention wandering around in a bikini top and hotpants than you would wearing a long skirt.

Being a female tourist (especially if you're young and blonde) will get you noticed regardless of what you're wearing, so feel free to put that maxi dress back in the wardrobe and wear normal clothes. You're probably going to get at least some verbal hassle anyway.

In Israel, not a day goes by without some sort of comment, wolf whistle or leery stare. Men will often ask for your email or phone number in the street, so make ready your fake number or fake boyfriend/husband or simply be assertive and tell them to leave you alone. For most female tourists, this is the most they have to deal with, but it helps to be a bit careful and aware when visiting here.

If you feel pressured or uncomfortable, ask a local woman for help. Many local women have to deal with this sort of shit every day so know exactly what to do and how to get rid of these idiots.

 Apart from that, the usual rules apply: don't go down dark streets (or quiet parks) on your own at night unless you know the area well and are feeling confident; don't accept a lift or a ride from a stranger and don't leave your drink unattended in the more commercial clubs (although cases of date rape are actually very rare in Tel Aviv). Some of the neighborhoods I've written about in this guide are not particularly "nice", but they are generally safer than similar neighborhoods abroad. Stick to the busier streets if you're uncertain and you should have no problem whatsoever.

Take care getting into taxis, as there have been some (rare) cases of dodgy drivers kidnapping and assaulting tourists. See the Taxi section for how to tell if a taxi belongs to a reputable company.

Oh and in case you're wondering, Tel Aviv's a modern city with western conveniences. There's no need to stock up on tampons before you arrive. If you're fed up of tampons and want to get your hands on a more environmentaly friendly, reusable femme cup while you're here (it's like a moon cup), you can email nitz.cups@gmail.com or visit http://www.fcup.co.il (Hebrew only).

LGBT

Nowhere in the Middle East (and Israel) is more open and relaxed about people's sexual preference than Tel Aviv. As part of the Israeli "pinkwashing" efforts, the city council does everything in its power to encourage gay tourism and there's a lot of money and effort being spent on making the city gay friendly. There are plenty of great bars, restaurants and guesthouses in town that are run by members of the *kehila* (meaning community, short for *Kehila Gea* or proud community, the Hebrew term for LGBT). That said, this is the Middle East we're talking about and Israelis are a fairly conservative (and macho) nation, all in all. Homophobia does exist, especially but not uniquely among religious people.

In general, public displays of affection between people of the same sex are very OK, but you may get some nasty looks from the more conservative types if you're unlucky. Outright homophobic violence is very rare.

I've noted a bunch of specifically gay and lesbian owned (or LGBT friendly) businesses within the guide. Because of the nature of this guide, I have ignored the more mainstream ones and went for the interesting alternative places, most of which are also straight-friendly.

For more information about gay Tel Aviv, including the mainstream stuff check out:

The Tel Aviv LGBT Community Center
http://gaycenter.org.il * office@gaycenter.org.il
Tchernihovsky 22A (entrance is from Gan Meir, which is between Tchernihovsky and King George St.) * 03-5252896

Everything from information, classes and workshops (yoga, art, music, etc.), cultural events, lectures and other useful stuff. There's also a weekly health clinic and sexual health clinic. There's a café here which serves as a useful meeting point and hangout but is otherwise not very exciting (nor cheap).

Gay Tel Aviv Guide: http://www.gaytlvguide.com

The Israeli GLBT Organisation: http://www.glbt.org.il

Israel's LGBT portal: http://gogay.co.il (Hebrew only)

You may also be interested in the following organisations:

Religious Jewish Gay Organisation: http://www.hod.org.il

Religious Jewish Lesbian Organisation: http://www.bat-kol.org

The Palestinian Arab Lesbian Organisation: http://www.aswatgroup.org/english

Events

Tel Aviv Gay Pride (Usually sometime in the first half of June.)

The Tel Aviv gay pride is a massively big deal and seems to get bigger every year. Apart from the outdoor events, the whole city explodes in parties for practically a whole week. Look up Tel Aviv Pride Parade on Facebook for a full list of events near the time.

Tel Aviv International LGBT Film Festival
http://www.tlvfest.com

A big annual festival of local and international LGBT interest movies. They also hold a monthly film club at the Cinemateque.

Lethal Lesbian (autumn)
http://lethallesbian.com/

Tel Aviv's dedicated Israeli lesbian film festival, showcasing some great local talent.

Sex

Men

I'll be blunt – if you're uncircumcised, many Israeli women won't want to have sex with you. The vast majority of Israeli women won't have seen an uncut penis in the flesh, but that doesn't stop many of them from not wanting to go near one. Don't take it personally, it's a Jewish thing. Not all local women are like that – many don't mind at all – but it's still common enough to be an issue. Don't make the mistake of thinking that because a woman is "alternative" (tattooed, pierced, funky) or appears cosmopolitan this won't be the case. Such women are more likely to not have a problem with your penis but there are no guarantees. On the gay scene, by the way, things are more relaxed (and safe sex more common).

Women

I'll be blunt again – many Israeli men are notoriously whiney about having to use condoms, especially now the morning after pill is readily available. Things are not as bad as they used to be, but carry your own protection if you're looking for action. Some guys will try very hard to convince you not to use a condom, but just think about all the other women they banged without one and then decide if your holiday romance is worth getting a disease. Genital warts affect the Chosen People too, as does AIDS, which is supposedly on the rise in Israel.

The local morning after pill is called **Postinor** (post-ee-norr) and is available over the counter from many private pharmacies and all SuperPharm branches. It costs around 100NIS.

Locations

Hapolaniya
Bograshov 29 * 03- 6202779 * Sun – Thur 11:00 – 21:00, Fri 10:00 – 16:00

A women-oriented sex shop with ultra-chic retro design and a good range of products for both women and men.

Sisters
http://sisters.co.il (Hebrew only)
Hangar 26, Tel Aviv port (inside Bait Banamal P. 166) * 03-5506678 * Sun – Thur 10:00- 23:00, Fri 10:00-16:00, Sat 11:00 – 23:00

A beautifully designed sex shop, part of a funky "department store" (see the Bait Banamal listing for more info). Lots of great stuff and good advice too.

Levinsky Anonymous Sexual Health Clinic
Central bus station building, 5th floor, store no. 5531 * 03-5373738 * Sun 16:00 – 2:00, Mon 13:00 – 17:00, Tues 15:30 – 20:00, Wed 13:00 -17:00, Thurs 9:00 – 12:30

For all your VD / STD needs. It's free. Call for an appointment or just turn up in case of an emergency.

Alcohol

The drinking age in Tel Aviv is 18. Prepare to show ID if you look young, although things are not always as strict as in, say, the USA. No alcoholic drinks can be bought from shops and supermarkets between 11PM and 6AM. Fines for store owners are huge, so they pretty much all comply and won't sell you booze within these times. If you want to drink during these times, go to a bar, a restaurant or a café. Outside of these times, you can buy alcohol practically everywhere, including most supermarkets, minimarkets and newsagents, plus fast food and street food places.

Although you can drink outdoors in the day, you're officially not allowed to be drinking outdoors in public spaces between 21:00 and 6:00. Sadly, this does include the beach. The police have the right to confiscate your alcohol if they find you drinking in a public space during those times (or at any other time if they believe you're causing a nuisance).

The government keeps hiking up taxes on cheap spirits but you can still get some cheap deals on vodka, as well as schnapps and arak (Lebanese ouzo), possibly the cheapest drinkable spirit in Israel (though sadly no longer cheap).

See the Buy Food. Eat Food chapter for some good places to buy booze.

Aniseed overdose

No Tel Aviv drinking experience is complete without a rough night on arak resulting in a lifelong hatred of anything to do with aniseed. The most common local varieties are all made by a single company – Emir HaArak (rare but the strongest), Elite HaArak (most common and very drinkable) and Aluf HaArak (fairly common and passably OK). Also try Zahlawi, which is considered of good quality. There are also some interesting Arab imports, though they are often more expensive and not that easy to get. Try the shops in Jaffa.

Cigarettes and the smoking ban

Everyone smokes in Tel Aviv. Cigarettes used to be a lot cheaper, but even with the increasing taxes they are cheaper than in most parts of Western Europe. You can get cigarettes in supermarkets, newsagents (where you can buy single cigarettes as well as packs) and in some bars and clubs.

There is an indoor smoking ban in Tel Aviv, though it isn't always strictly enforced. Cafés and restaurants generally enforce it, though in winter you will often have an enclosed, covered smokers' area that is essentially another room, rather than a cold, windswept garden. When the weather gets nicer, smokers just sit outside. Bars and clubs are often more lenient, often against the law. This is bad news for non-smokers, especially in the more underground places covered in this guide. Some bars and clubs do enforce it, though, and I've pointed that out in the listings.

If you're intent on smoking indoors, pay close attention to what the locals are doing and follow suit. Inspectors have the power to give you big spot fines, so if everyone in the venue starts throwing their half-lit cigarettes on the floor, you should probably do the same or face the consequences.

Drugs

Drugs are very very illegal in Israel, though you won't get your arms chopped off for taking them. In fact, lots and lots of people smoke weed in Tel Aviv, usually homegrown grass or medical weed, though there are occasionally imports of hash from Jordan and Egypt. The party scene obviously has its fair share of things like LSD (liquid and tabs), pills and MDMA.

Penalties for drug offenses in Tel Aviv are generally tamer than in other parts of Israel, but as a foreigner you may still get screwed.

Entrapment is legal in Israel and undercover policemen often infiltrate parties to try and do people. Take extra care if you're heading out of town for a "nature party" (semi-legal or illegal rave) where the police can get far nastier and penalties can be more severe (jail time). Even in Tel Aviv policemen can get rather nasty at illegal parties, though more in a kick your ass way than land you in jail for drugs way.

Tel Aviv has a thriving trade of all kinds of legal highs. Some of these are reputedly quite strong and can reportedly be quite realistic. Most are pretty vile with nasty side effects. The shops selling them pop up every once in a while in places like Florentin (usually Florentin St. or Frenkel St., west of Herzl) and along the northern end of Allenby street (before it turns towards the sea) and have opaque, colourful fronts with psychedelic pictures or Jamaican coloured cartoons. Some newsagents also sell them. They usually come as "incense" or "herbal tea".

For more information about how evil drug users score actual weed in Tel Aviv, you can visit: http://www.webehigh.org and check out their city guide for Tel Aviv. Obviously, this is for novelty value only. DIY Tel Aviv does not condone illegal activity of any kind.

By the way, khat, locally known as gat, is 100% legal in Israel in its fresh form. Chewing it gives a mild speedy buzz (read more about it at http://en.wikipedia.org/wiki/Khat). To sample this popular natural high, head to the Tikva Market or the Yemenite Quarter (Kerem Hateimanim) where you can usually buy the fresh leaves. The juice made from the leaves recently became illegal, but some places may still be selling it. Try **Rina & Zecharia's** at 22 Hakovshim St. (Yemenite quarter). This is a crumbling and very authentic Yemenite restaurant run by an old couple who were the first to dish out the juice, which is said to give you vitality and focus. Note that this is not a stoner's café but more or a workers' restaurant serving cheap stews and soups (amazing if you're into meat, otherwise, not so much). Gat is as acceptable as coffee in Yemenite culture and the owners are old and somewhat conservative.

You can also get bottles of arak infused with khat leaves in some places. The ingredients are often listed in Hebrew only. Make of that what you will. Try Florentin Drinks on Florentin 14, where there's a good range of other types of flavoured araks (though you can get those elsewhere as well).

Gat Eden (http://www.shotgat.com Hebrew only) is an organic farming collective that sells both locally grown organic gat and Ethiopian gat flown in three times a week. They supply all over central Israel, including Tel Aviv. Call 050-3533533 or 08-9357889 to find your local supplier. Haggling over the price won't hurt.

2 Sleep

Accommodation can be the most expensive part of staying in Tel Aviv, but it doesn't have to be a total killer. As this is an alternative / cultural guide, I've not researched hundreds of hotels and hostels, but have included a few places that are special or good value (or both), as well as alternative accommodation options. I find www.tripadvisor.com a good up to date resource for hotels and hostels, so if you can't get a room at the places below, you can check there as well.

Here's a quick breakdown of your options:

Hotels are expensive in Tel Aviv and I would say most are not good value compared to some other cities. Expect to pay around $120+ a night for a livable hotel and over $150 for a nice one. **Hostels** in Tel Aviv are often shabby and not that cheap but private rooms are a lot cheaper than rooms in hotels. **Holiday flats** are generally better value than hotels and are cheaper per night/week. They are often more expensive than **Sublets** which are actually quite plentiful in town (both rooms in shared flats and whole flats). People sublet places for anything from a week to several months and you can sometimes even find deals for a few days. You can also **rent a room in someone's flat** (rather than sublet someone's room), which is often more expensive than a sublet as it's aimed at tourists. You may expect such rooms and flats to be more geared towards tourists in class too, but in Tel Aviv that is not always the case. It might feel more like being someone's lodger in a normal flat, for better or worse. Of course, there's always **Couchsurfing**, if you want to stay for free (see end of chapter).

Hotels

Cheap and cool

Sun Hotels (http://www.sun-hotels.co.il) is a chain of 3 boutique cheapies. Their hotels are very basic but clean and slightly more interesting than your average cheapie, with some good locations too. The **Galileo Hotel** is my favourite and is in the cool surroundings of the Yemenite Quarter, seconds away from the Carmel market, minutes from the beach and next door to a cool bar. It has retro furniture and a cool rooftop, plus some rooms have Jacuzzis. The **Sun City Hotel** is very well located on Allenby St. but is noisier and less stylish. The **Port Hotel** is a bit far from the action (unless you're into the overpriced, mainstream nightlife offered by the port area itself) but sweet nonetheless.

Eden House (http://www.edenhousetlv.com)
Kehilat Eden 27 * 052-7469842 * moidrug@gmail.com

A small guest house with cute rooms decorated in proper Tel Aviv style. It's chilled and pretty and comes highly recommended. The location in the Yemenite Quarter is perfect for the beach, the Carmel Market and anywhere else (while still being very peaceful) and the owners are incredibly helpful.

Decent but dull

Maxim Hotel
http://www.maxim-htl-ta.co.il
Hayarkon 86 * 03-5173721

Pleasant enough with clean, modern rooms and the price is OK for Tel Aviv. This one is in the main tourist area of town, but overlooks the sea and is close to the excellent transport links of

Ben Yehuda St. so can be a good base to explore even the more exciting underground quarters.

Olympia Hotel
(book through Expedia.com and places like that) * HaYarkon 164 * 03-5242184 * olympiareserv@bezeqint.net

Clean, not entirely basic and generally reasonably priced. It's in the main tourist area of town and close to the beach. It's really not a very exciting place to stay but good if the cooler places are booked up and you just want a place to rest your head at night.

Reasonably priced boutiques

Atlas Hotels (http://www.atlas.co.il) is a chain of very tasteful Israeli boutique hotels that has quite a few very cool hotels around Tel Aviv. They're not cheap (around 600NIS+ a night) but this is the least you'd pay for a properly "nice" hotel in Tel Aviv. **Cinema Hotel** and **Center Hotel** are based in pretty old Bauhaus buildings in the very central and handy Dizengoff Square, while their other offerings (**Tal, Shalom, Melody and Art+**) are in the main tourist areas of Ben Yehuda and Hayarkon streets in more modern buildings. Rooms are often smallish but very well-decorated in a fun, modern way or a more retro style.

Hostels

Old Jaffa Hostel
http://www.inisrael.com/oldjaffahostel
Amiad 13, Jaffa * 03-6822316, 03-6822370 * ojhostel@shani.net

Set in an old building, this is probably the most scenic / romantic hostel in town. It offers painted floors, high ceilings, ancient bricks and a great vibe. Their huge roof terrace is a true legend and affords both sea views and flea market views. The location is perfect for both Jaffa and Tel Aviv's more happening southern neighbourhoods like Florentin. Great nightlife is guaranteed, as the area has most of the city's most exciting bars.

The Carmel Hostel
Hacarmel 17 (slightly down the cross alleyway) * 03-5160821 * 050-5686098

This place is clean but basic and shabby-looking, decorated in a somewhat tacky Middle Eastern style. On the other hand, it's in one of the best locations in town, literally right on the very central Carmel market. The rooms are surprisingly quiet for such a busy and exciting place. It's very cheap: around 200NIS for a double room with air conditioning, a private bathroom and a small fridge (though you may need to haggle). There's no kitchen or a communal dining hall and this place is very old school – I couldn't find reference to it online and there's no WiFi or Internet on site. If you can't find a free network, use the awesome **Little Prince café** at Nahalat Binyamin 18, or the **LovEat** place on Nahalat Binyamin 3 to get online (there's also a PC you can use at the newsagent/minimarket at Allenby 58).

Chef Hostel
http://www.chefhostel.com
Montefiore 19 (ground floor, the door on the right. No sign) * 052-2895145 * chefhostel@gmail.com

A family run hostel in a great central-south location - minutes away from cool nightlife, cafés and the Nahalat Binyamin pedestrianised area. Rooms and dorms are basic but comfortable and the place feels like staying with a friendly family with the added benefit of having gourmet meals and BBQs cooked for you on occasion.

Self-catering holiday flats

Flats vary greatly in price and level of poshness, so it helps to shop around (and haggle). Some of the more expensive ones are done up like 5 star hotels, while others are (sometimes) cheaper but older and shabbier. The flats usually come equipped with everything you need to stay and cook in the place. Most now have wireless Internet and some will even have computers you can use.

I've listed a few cool flats below. I recommend contacting them well in advance as they can book up fast, especially during the busy spring and summer seasons.

To find more flats, you can look in **online noticeboards** like Tel Aviv Craig's list (telaviv.craigslist.org) which is in English, http://www.airbnb.com (English/International) and also in http://www.homeless.co.il/shortterm which has both Hebrew and English ads.

There are also a few more organised **flat rental services** where you can find flats, which are often more upmarket/expensive, but you can sometimes get good deals (haggle!). These companies also offer other services such as transfers, car or bicycle rental and even mobile phones and laundry services. These are great for convenience, but note that you can often get those extra services cheaper if you go direct. Some good companies to try are: http://www.tlv2go.com, http://www.stayatmyplace.co.il and http://telavivapts.net. They also offer holiday flats for other cities In Israel.

Watch out for creative interpretations of "central Tel Aviv". Some ads on Craig's list, for example, are actually for places outside of Tel Aviv (Givatayim, Herzelia, Hod Hasharon and even Netanya), or in neighbourhoods that are considered pretty far from the centre (Yad Eliyahu, for example). Ask for an exact address and use your Google map before agreeing to anything. In Tel Aviv, anything east of the Ayalon freeway or north of the Yarkon river is considered too far from the action by most visitors and the eastern neighbourhoods in particular won't be to everyone's liking. I cannot stress this enough: prices quoted for tourists are always, always higher than they would be for Israelis. It's always worth trying to haggle, especially in the low season or if you're going to stay for a week or longer.

Tali's flat

http://on.fb.me/FPYnul for pics
htali11@yahoo.com * 03-5229261

A large, secure and beautiful 2 bedroom (3 room) flat (one double, one single) in the centre of town (Dizengoff / Frishman area) with a sweet garden, a huge bath, washing machine, microwave and everything else you might need. It sleeps 4-5 adults or 4 adults and a child (one double bed in the bedroom, one double sofa bed in the huge open plan lounge, plus a single mattress on the floor in the single room). Costs around 500NIS a night.

Edna's flat

ednakedar@gmail.com

A lovely and spacious 1 bedroom (2 room) flat on a quiet street in the quiet and very desirable Sheinkin area (Borochov St.). It's decorated in an artistic shabby-chic style and has a cute little balcony and everything you need to live, cook and work. Perfect for a couple or a single person, but there's plenty of space (and mattresses) for at least two more people to sleep in the lounge if you want. Costs around 450NIS per night for single occupancy, 50NIS per additional person. Reduced rates for weekly or monthly rental.

Yael's Flat

yaelcanbefound@gmail.com

I've not been to this flat myself, but it's apparently it's a 1 bed (2 room) flat in the trendy Gan Hachashmal area (centre-south). It's a great location for transport, nightlife and shopping but can get noisy. A great deal at around 180NIS per night with significant rate reductions for longer periods.

Sublets

Sublets are often a good deal but are not particularly geared for tourists, so you may have to lower your standards a bit or have less room for your own gear. Tel Aviv residents travel often, so there are usually lots of opportunities, especially around major holidays when lots of people go away. Apart from the places already noted above in the holiday flats section, there are some Facebook groups you can look in or post your own ad:

English groups:

Secret Tel Aviv (which is also a good place to ask any other question about life in Tel Aviv)

Home Exchange Israel-Europe

Home Exchange Israel-USA

Home Exchange Israel: Sublets only

Kosher Home Exchange

http://on.fb.me/Ze4B2c (Hebrew and English, long and short term)

(Mostly) Hebrew groups where you can post in English and ask:

http://www.facebook.com/groups/36672129795/

http://www.facebook.com/groups/45245752193/

I also have a noticeboard on the DIY Tel Aviv site where I occasionally post ads for sublets.

Note that many people only post up the ads once they've tried going the friends / friends of friends route, so you often have more of a chance of finding somewhere last minute than you do, say, 5, 3 or even one month in advance.

Word of advice – if at all possible, avoid getting a ground floor flat. Burglaries are very common, especially in the Southern neighbourhoods, and the ground floor is the most commonly targeted location. Ground floor places are often cheaper, but only go for one if the windows all have fixed bars and the door is a strong one with a proper lock (these doors are called "Pladellet" here, as that is one company that makes them). Top floor flats with balconies in buildings with easy access to the roof and no locked main entry door can also be at increased risk.

If you're looking for **long term sublets / rentals,** note that the Hebrew groups (and, sometimes, Craigslist) are also good for those. All the groups have discussion boards as well where more ads are regularly posted.

Stay with locals

Pay to stay

Here are a few of people I know of who rent rooms in their flats on a short term basis. Remember that all prices in Israel are negotiable, especially in the low season or if you're staying for a while. Staying in someone's flat in Tel Aviv is more like being a temporary lodger than staying in a B&B. Expect most flats to be "lived in" (i.e. somewhat messy) at best.

Assaf's Flat
https://www.airbnb.com/rooms/514934

A big and comfortable room with a small enclosed balcony in this clean flat located near Rabin Square. The friendly hosts provides handy extras like a phone with a local sim card and even a tablet computer you can use while you're here.

Noa's flat
kram.noa@gmail.com

A small but bright room with a single bed and storage space in a pleasant and peaceful shabby chic flat on the brilliantly located Geula St. (great for the beach, the Carmel market and public transport). The host is a friendly and well-travelled postgraduate lady student in her late 30s who's looking for mature and respectful guests. The room costs 140NIS per night, or you could rent on a weekly or monthly basis as well.

Ilanit's flat
ilaniterez@gmail.com

A friendly and welcoming place to stay - a comfortable room with a double bed, air conditioning and wardrobe space in a very well located flat on a quiet street just behind Dizengoff Center (and minutes from the beach). The artistic and interesting host is a single mother to a sweet home schooled little girl (6 years old at the time of writing) and the flat also has a cute little dog. The condition of the flat is lived in at best and raising a toddler can be a crazy job, so don't expect hotel standard living, but the location is perfect and the flat (and hosts) are super friendly. There's fast WiFi, a great bathroom with a big bath and use of the kitchen. Price is 150NIS (negotiable) with discounts for longer stays.

Yael's Flat
yaelcanbefound@gmail.com

I've not seen this place myself yet, but it sounds good: two separate rooms you can rent in a big flat shared with a local lady. Weekly (700NIS) or monthly (2750NIS) rental options available, with all bills included. The location is the trendy Gan Hachashmal area (centre-south), with cool designer stores plus trendy cafés, restaurants and nightlife. It can get a bit noisy though, plus is about 30 minutes' walk to the beach.

Ruti's Flat
rut.stern.klein@gmail.com

Not central, but lovely, chilled and cheap - only 100NIS a night. You'd be staying in a flat with the friendly host plus her 3 cool school-aged daughters who stay some of the time. The flat is big and bright, on a quiet street in the rundown Hatikva neighbourhood (east of the Ayalon highway). There are good 24 hour transport links to the centre, plus a nearby train to the

University. The neighbourhood has an awesome market, good food and some fun cheap stores, but it's neither central nor "nice" to look at and although it's generally safe, may be a bit too "third world" for some people. The flat itself is certainly a home, not a hotel, which I personally love, and sleeping is on mattresses on the floor in a room that has a big frosted glass door instead of one of its walls. Still, if you want to meet some really cool people in a truly welcoming place and see some sides of Tel Aviv most tourists will never see, then you'll love it.

Rina's flat
rina.sade@gmail.com

The flat is in the Yad Eliyahu neighbourhood (east of the Ayalon highway), which is not central, but close enough to public transport to have you in the centre of town in 10 minutes or so once you're on the bus. The room is small, with a queen sized bed and a wardrobe, and there's full use of a big kitchen, a lounge and everything else (washing machine, internet, etc.). The room can be rented on a daily, weekly or monthly basis. The rate per night is $40. Good if you want a quiet place.

For more rooms, check out airbnb.com, telaviv.craigslist.org or the subletting Facebook groups above (especially the Hebrew ones).

Stay for free

http://www.couchsurfing.com has a very big Israeli / Tel Aviv presence, so it's worth registering and looking on the site if the thought of spending a few nights on friendly people's sofas appeals. Unlike AirBnB, couchsurfing arrangements are free and the Tel Aviv community is on the whole very welcoming. Most people will host for a night or two, but sometimes you can get a sofa for longer periods. Plan ahead and you could easily stay in Tel Aviv for free for your entire trip.

Women should note that while the majority of Israeli male couchsurfing hosts are very nice, Israeli men have a thing for foreign ladies. It's up to you whether you want to stay only with women (there are plenty to choose from) or stay with guys as well and hope you get a nice one, but I would suggest avoiding it unless you're worldly and well traveled and know you can handle unwanted advances from hosts should the situation arise. To be fair, I should say that in general I personally don't like staying with male hosts when I travel anywhere in the world, because I've heard enough stories to make me want to sidestep the issue altogether. On the other hand, Israeli men are the only ones I've personally come across who consistently use Couchsurfing to try and chat up random women, which to me does not bode well for actually staying with them (unless you're also looking for sex).

3 Get around

Cycling

Cycling is by far the best way to get around Tel Aviv, and if you want to get into the swing of things and feel like a local, I suggest you get on a bike, even if it's only for a few hours of casual sightseeing along the Tayelet.

But why stop there? If you're spending any significant length of time in town, you may as well go local and get yourself a pair of wheels, bypassing annoying taxi drivers, gridlocked traffic and slow-moving pedestrians and staying green and healthy while you're at it. The city is mostly flat and the weather is usually nice, though heat can be an issue for some throughout the year.

Cycling in Tel Aviv is not for everyone, though. Tel Aviv isn't Amsterdam and cycle paths are still relatively few and far between. Those paths that do exist are often infested with clueless pedestrians with zero spatial awareness and a tendency to walk in zigzags. A loud bell and an itchy trigger finger might help and you'll also need either saintly patience or nerves of steel.

The main (and most pleasant) cycle paths are along Tel Aviv's boulevards – Rothschild, Ben Gurion, Nordau, Chen and Ben Zion. There are also paths on both sides of Ibn Gabirol Street and, of course, along the seafront – the Tayelet.

Officially, you're meant to wear a helmet when you cycle and you're not meant to cycle on the pavement (sidewalk). In reality, these laws are not enforced. You'll hardly see anyone wearing a helmet in town and people cycle on the pavement all the time, which I suggest you also do, unless you're a shit hot cyclist. Most people don't even know you're supposed to only cycle on the road and on bike paths. Hell, most people don't even use bike lights at night and no one cares. Basically, the only way you'd get in trouble with the police while cycling is if you cycled right into a cop and knocked him over. Of course, I would never encourage you to break the law in any way and the helmet is there for your own safety, so don't sue me if you fall off a bike and hurt yourself.

Israeli drivers often get confused when they see cyclists on the road as most bikers here use the pavement. If you cycle on the road, you're likely to get people driving slowly behind you and honking their horn to make you get out of the way. They are usually too scared to overtake, even if there's lots of room.

Getting a bike – the public bike rental scheme

Tel Aviv has a public bike rental scheme called **Tel-O-Fun** (https://www.tel-o-fun.co.il). While annoying problems are pretty common (bikes not being released from docking stations, returned bikes not being registered as returned, etc.), it's still one of the best ways to get around town or enjoy a leisurely ride along the beach.

As a tourist, you will likely want to use the daily and weekly membership options which you can easily sign up to with most foreign credit cards at any docking station around town. If you're staying in town for a while or moving here, the yearly membership option may be useful, which you can sign up to on their website.

The cute green bikes are equipped with lights and bells, as well as a handy rack on the back (which makes them about a 100 times better than most bikes in town). There are English menus at the docking stations, making rental relatively easy. You basically get a daily membership to the scheme for 17NIS (23NIS on Saturdays and holidays) or a weekly one for 60NIS to use the bikes. With your membership, using any bike anywhere is free for the first half hour. If you go over into the next half hour, you pay 5NIS and the next half hour will cost another 5NIS. From then on things get more expensive: 20NIS for the next half hour, 40NIS for the next and so on, ending at 1200NIS per 24 hours.

The bikes are basically meant for short trips between docking stations, rather than a lengthy journey. With this in mind, if you're thinking of bringing your bike back to a station, logging it in and then taking it (or another bike) out straight away to continue your sojourn for free, you'll need to wait 10 minutes in between rentals. If a docking station is full – you should still attempt to check in there. It will direct you to nearby stations and give you extra time to get there.

Note that the fines for losing a bike are huge (4500NIS), even if the bike gets stolen. Always check it into a station if you're not using it.

The Tel-O-Fun website has some useful info in English about how to use the bikes, but their map of the stations was in Hebrew only last time I checked. I made my own map in English you can use instead. It lives here: http://bit.ly/la0UuE

The council gives out free Hebrew and English maps of the rental stations, which you can get at the tourist offices, big hotels / tourist attractions and some branches of McDonald's in Tel Aviv.

If this all sounds too complicated, there are also places around town that rent standard bikes specifically to tourists (see below).

Buying a (cheap) bike

If you want a dedicated, guaranteed bike for a week or more and are not precious about the quality of your vehicle, you should know that you can actually buy cheap used bikes from as little as 250 NIS. Remember that a cheap bike in Tel Aviv is usually either shit or stolen (or both). Some places do trade in deals and will sell you those old bikes cheaply, but any bike you get won't be that great. If you're precious, go for the rentals, though the quality of those isn't guaranteed either.

If you're buying a used bike, you'll need a lock, which can set you back another 30 NIS for a cheap one (not so good) or around 70 NIS or more for a decent one (better).

Tel Aviv Craig's list (telaviv.craigslist.org) or Facebook group Secret Tel Aviv are the best places to try for cheap bikes sold by departing foreigners. On Secret Tel Aviv you can sometimes rent or borrow a bike as well. Those often come with a lock and sometimes with other accessories too. You might want to ask the seller where they got the bike, though, cause some may have unknowingly bought a stolen one.

Be suspicious of any used bike bought in Jaffa (especially the flea market), the Neve Shaanan market and anywhere south of Levinsky Street. All bikes sold on Neve Shaanan St. in the old bus station area or in the Jaffa flea market are pretty much guaranteed to be stolen goods. Please don't support junkies and thieves by buying from the people who pay them.

If that's not enough to put you off buying stolen goods, remember that Tel Aviv is all in all a very small place and people do recognise their stolen bikes on the street and will either steal them back or lock them down and contact the police.

Getting a bike if you're in town for longer periods

If you're here for work or study, you may well want to buy a nicer set of wheels than the crap you can get for 250NIS. Good used bikes start at around 400NIS and you can usually get passable new bikes from not much more than that. Head to the south of town for the better deals on new bikes, as prices are significantly lower there. For good used bikes, it's worth checking the more northern stores as well, as people are likely to trade in better bikes there.

Word of advice if you're buying a nice bike – if you want it to keep, get yourself a can of nasty-looking spray paint and cover up any bit of niceness that would make your bike look in any way desirable. Yes, I know it hurts, but it does mean your bike will be less likely to get stolen, especially if you live in the southern parts of town. You could also try painting it a mad colour and making it very distinctive instead. Either that or keep your bike in the flat with you overnight.

Getting rid of your bike when you leave

- Bring it back to the same shop you bought it from and sell it back to them

- Take it to a different shop that sells second-hand bikes (you might get a better deal then)

- Give it to someone nice you met at your hostel or hotel
- Advertise it for sale on Craig's list (English only), homeless.co.il (Hebrew only) or yad2.co.il (Hebrew only) if you have the time to wait and deal with it

- Give it to a good cause – **Pitchon Lev** is a charity that collects donations of all sorts (food, clothes, toys, household appliances and yes, bicycles too). They are always keen. Donations are passed onto the needy (regardless of race, religion, etc.) and anything that's either damaged or otherwise unwanted is sold in their charity shop to the public at low prices. Their collection point and shop is a short walk from both the central bus station and HaHagana train station, making getting back easy. Their details are: http://pitchonlev.org.il * Golomb 54 * 03-5377760 * Sun 9:00 – 19:00, Mon – Wed 10:00 – 19:00, Thurs 9:00 – 14:00

Bike shops and rental places

O-fun
http://o-fun.co.il
Ben Yehuda 197 * Phone: 03-5442292 * Email:
ofun.rentals@gmail.com * Sun – Thurs 10:00 – 19:00, Fri 10:00 –
14:00

A friendly, well-stocked store and rental place with a giant fleet of
mountain and city bikes, all with a very obvious O-fun logo, which
may somewhat detract from your attempt to blend in, but may
make a thief hesitate slightly. They rent out on an hourly, daily
and weekly basis. Prices are 25NIS an hour, 60NIS a day. Check
for weekly rate. They also rent out tandem bikes at 110NIS a day
and mopeds /scooters for 150NIS a day.

Bicikef
Yehuda Levi 49 * 074-7015050 * Sun - Fro 12:00 – 18:00

This nice guy seems to always have quality used bikes in store at
very reasonable prices. He also does repairs and sells new bikes.

Cycle
http://cycle.co.il
Ben Yehuda 147 * Phone: 03-5293037 * Email:
udiyahav@hotmail.com * Sun – Thurs 10:00 – 19:00, Fri 10:00 –
15:00

They mostly rent out mountain bikes, but can also accommodate
some special requests (city bikes, road bikes, etc.). Rates are
currently 25NIS an hour and 55NIS a day. They also sell used
bikes. The used bikes they sell are all brought in as part of trade
in deals, so not pre-stolen.

Wheel Bee
http://www.wheelbeetlv.com
Hahalfanim 7 (Corner of Yefet 12), Jaffa * 03-6838080 * Sun –
Thur 9:00-18:00 (19:30 in summer), Fri 9:00 – 14:00(15:30 in
summer), Sat 9:30 – 18:00

A handy place to rent a bike from in Jaffa, though not cheap. They have a good selection of all kinds of bikes, from simple mountain bikes, cruisers and city bikes to tandems, electric bikes, kids' bikes and "half bikes". From 75NIS per day (55NIS per 6 hours).

My Bike
Rothschild 84 * 050 – 2245348
Sun – Thurs 10:00 – 19:00, Fri 10:00 – 14:00 (flexible).

Regularly have cheap (250NIS and up) used bikes for sale and also sometimes rent out old refurbished bikes on an hourly, daily or weekly basis at reduced rates (stock permitting). The place is run by die-hard, cool cycle enthusiast dudes who never knowingly buy stolen goods. They also offer surprisingly good deals on repairs, considering the posh location, more expensive than South Tel Aviv, but they generally do better work.

Tel Aviv Bikes
http://tlv-bikes.co.il (Hebrew only)
Pinsker 62 * 03 – 6205104 * Sun – Thurs 10:00 – 19:00, Fri 10:00 – 14:30

Really friendly, knowledgeable guys offering good deals on repairs and accessories. They sell reasonably priced new bikes and occasionally have special deals on mountain bikes with some pretty cheap offers. Not particularly useful to a short-term tourist unless your bike breaks down near them, but I have only good things to say about this place so figured it's worth mentioning in case you're in town for longer.

Shahaf Bikes
http://www.sbikes.co.il (Hebrew only)
Levinsky 80 * 03-6884734 * Sun – Fri

My favourite out of the many cheap bicycle stores that are dotted throughout this stretch of Levinsky (between HaAliya and Har Zion). Nice guys offering very cheap repairs, cheap new bikes and the occasional second hand bike. If they don't have what you're after, one of the other stores on the street will.

Some hotels, such as **Cinema Hotel** and **Center Hotel** (see hotel section) have a bunch of free bikes for their guests to use.

Events

Critical Mass is a monthly gathering of cyclists celebrated in many cities around the world. Cyclists meet at a pre-arranged location and head off en mass to explore the city and promote cycling as a fun, healthy, environmentally friendly activity. It's a great way to meet like-minded people and see the city. The Tel Aviv ride often leads on to a party or another eco-friendly event, so be sure to ask around.

The **Tel Aviv Critical Mass** meets every last Friday of the month at 13:30 at Rabin Square. Their (rarely updated) website is at http://criticalmasstlv.wordpress.com/ and there is also a (slightly more active) Facebook group, aptly named "Critical Mass Tel Aviv". As the days become intolerably hot for summer, the rides become less reliable, but they return around September and carry on through winter (but not on rainy days).

Cyclists now also join the weekly **Tuesday night Tel Aviv Rollers ride** that meets at 21:30 at the top of Ben Zion Blvd. (by Habima Theatre) and heads off around 22:00 for a fun and thrilling ride around town. Please be considerate and ride behind the skaters. Also, note that Israelis hate rainy weather, so if it's forecast to rain, the ride will be moved. For routes, dates and any changes check on their Facebook group (TAR – Tel Aviv Rollers) in the discussion section where there are English listings. Try a few days in advance, as the ride is sometimes moved to the Monday before when rain is forecast for the Tuesday.

Ecobike (http://www.ecobike.co.il/) is a bike tour company that runs regular guided tours of Tel Aviv (bring your own bike). Some of them are free. Check their site for more info.

Roller blades / skateboards

Currently, the only place that rents out rollerblades in town is the Tel Aviv Sportek in Park Hayarkon. Their equipment is reportedly somewhat crap and the place shuts at 21:00, rendering it useless for providing you with a way to attend the weekly ride (see cycling events above).

For rollerblade equipment, parts and repairs, try EndlessRoll (http://www.endlessroll.com).

Tel Aviv now has a roller derby team. Check out their Facebook page at http://www.facebook.com/TLVDerbyGirls for more info.

Apart from the Tuesday night ride listed above, there is also a weekly sunset ride on Fridays that meets at the **Sportek** in Hayarkon Park (16:30 during winter, 17:30 in summer). The (Hebrew) route and change announcements are at:

http://bit.ly/JbYaU9 or you can try asking in the TAR – Tel Aviv Rollers Facebook group.

Cars

Driving in Tel Aviv is traffic hell and parking is even worse. Unfortunately, if you're thinking of getting out of town for the weekend at any point, you'll need a car to get there. Otherwise, you'll face Israel's somewhat sub-optimal public transport system which doesn't run on Shabat. It involves only shared taxis going to and from major cities and expensive private ("special") taxis.

Most of the big international rental companies have a presence in Tel Aviv, so you could try hertz.co.il , avis.co.il, budget.co.il, etc. The biggest local company is **Eldan** (http://www.eldan.co.il) and there are a few other ones along haYarkon street all within walking distance of each other (www.shlomo.co.il, www.auto-shay.com, etc.).

The Israeli companies are often cheaper than the international ones, but watch out for dirty tricks. Sometimes a branch could run out of your class of car but try to tempt you with an upgrade (for an additional fee) rather than just give you the better car straight away. If you politely refuse an upgrade, you may well get the better car anyway, and at no extra cost.

All the branches in town are shut on Shabat. The airport branches are open 24/7, but you get charged around $30 more if you pick up or drop off there. It's important (and annoying) to note that the only way to get to and from the airport on Shabat without a car is with a private taxi.

Calauto (www.calauto.co.il) and Suncar (www.suncar.co.il) do cheap deals on last minute and one day rentals. Calauto even have a branch at the little Sde Dov airport in north Tel Aviv that's open till 19:00 on Fridays and till 23:00 in the week (sadly, no longer on Saturdays) and offer mostly small cars. Suncar seem to be the cheapest for one day rentals and also cheap for weekend rentals. You may also want to try the Israeli car2go (car2go.co.il) for hourly rentals (good for short distances / periods but requires a subscription).

As far as I know, you don't get charged one way rental fees in Israel, though if you try to return in Eilat or somewhere similarly distant, things may be different.

As for parking, there are many paid car parks scattered throughout the city but they are not cheap. There is a big selection of car parks along the beach, off Hayarkon St. Your rental place will be able to advise you further on ones near you. Ask about free car parks, as well, as there are a few, including The Reading West car park in the north (Rokach 7) and the Elifelet car park on Elifelet St. just west of Florentin.

In Israel, white markings on the pavement mean residents only, red and white markings mean no parking and blue and white markings mean parking is allowed with use of a parking ticket or rechargeable electronic parking passes (these can officially only be bought from machines in the post office). Normally, you are allowed to park by the blue and white markings overnight till about 7:00 or 8:00AM, but watch out for (Hebrew) signs saying otherwise. Hours vary across town and some roads have additional residents only restrictions. Red and yellow markings are for bus stops, which you can park at when the buses are not running: namely Friday evening till Saturday evening and those holidays that are like a Shabat.

Motorbikes and mopeds

You need a bike license to ride any bike or moped in Israel. Israeli drivers are aggressive and not very bike-aware so you'll also need to be quite confident on a bike to manage. The helmet law is very strictly enforced and rightly so. Many people die here every year in bike-related accidents.

Tel Aviv mopeds are everywhere – on the pavement, the wrong way down one-way streets, etc. as if they were bloody bicycles. Although common, this is very illegal and cops will give you huge spot fines if they catch you doing it. So don't.

Getting a bike or a moped

Motogo (http://www.motogo.co.il * 03 – 6811717) rent out 125cc bikes. **O-fun** (see Cycling section) also rent out mopeds.

Segways

If you want to cruise the town in (questionable) style, **Eldan** (see the car section) currently rent out Segways by the hour. They're fun for a tour of the seafront but I'm not sure where else you can go with them.

Taxis

All Taxis in Tel Aviv have yellow Taxi signs on top. The signs don't switch off when the taxi's picked up a fare, which is often a cause of some frustration. Those taxis that are a part of a reputable taxi company also have a little flag on top with the name of the company they belong to. If you want to be absolutely safe, never get into a cab that doesn't have a flag. This is especially important if you are a woman traveling solo (or with another female friend) as there are occasionally stories about dodgy taxi drivers trying to kidnap women. It's rare, but it does happen and young tourists are usually the victims when it does. I would suggest you don't risk it: it's better to wait a few more minutes for a reputable taxi than to end up in a sticky situation. In most cards you pay with cash. Some companies have card facilities, but don't count on it.

If you want to order a cab rather than hail one, here are the two biggest companies that operate 24/7:

Kastel Taxis
http://www.kastel.co.il
03 - 6991296 / 8

Shekem Taxis
03-6720800
03 – 5270404

You can also use a free smartphone app called **Get Taxi**, which is connected to a number of regulated companies in Tel Aviv and allows you to pay for your taxi by either card or cash.

Taxis are metered and should be using the meter. They may try to "cut you a deal" (read – "cheat the stupid tourist out of more money than the ride's worth"), but unless you know the route and how much the ride is meant to cost, it's best not to agree to it. Tipping is not required either way.

Buses

There are several bus companies that serve Tel Aviv. The main two are **Dan** (http://www.dan.co.il) and **Egged** (http://www.egged.co.il). Dan buses are of various colours, all marked with the wheeled Dan logo. They provide the main transport links within Tel Aviv itself and to its neighbouring towns. Egged buses are usually green and coach-like and provide the main intercity transport. They mostly leave from the central bus station, but some have stops in other parts of town. Another bus company is **Kavim** (http://www.kavim-t.co.il, which also serves neighbouring cities. It's not likey to be of much interest to the casual tourist, but it's worth noting their logo, so that you know the difference between their buses and the Dan ones. Another bus company that leaves from the central bus station is **Metropoline** (http://www.metropoline.com, Hebrew only). It serves the south of Israel and the Sharon and some of its buses have WiFi.

The Dan network has just had a major overhaul, so information in English about the bus lines may be a bit unreliable. There is a new website detailing the changes (http://busline.co.il) but it's in Hebrew only. The Dan website itself is somewhat of a pain to use in English (and Hebrew).

An unofficial site, http://www.otobusim.co.il aims to provide info on all buses and trains in Israel and has a reasonable English section, so you can try that instead.

The main bus routes you'll want to know are:

5 – From the Central train station to the central bus station along Dizengoff, Rothschild and a little bit of Allenby.

4 – From the Reading power station along Ben Yehuda St. and Allenby to the Central Bus Station.

18 – From the Central train station to Bat Yam via Ibn Gabirol, King George, Allenby, The Carmel Market, the south end of the Tayelet and Jaffa. It then carries on to Bat Yam, a neighbouring town.

25 – The main line going to the Tel Aviv University: starts outside Tel Aviv in the neighbouring Bat Yam, goes along Sderot Yerushalaim in Jaffa, then along Salame to Ha'Aliya, Allenby, King George, Ibn Gabirol and onto Ramat Aviv for the Uni.

72/172 – A new line replacing old lines 1 and 2. Good for getting to the top edge of Florentin from the North of town, along Allenby and Ben Yehuda.

23 - A little red minibus line that goes from Dizengoff and Sheinkin to the Azrieli shopping centre and Hashalom train station.

The Tel Aviv Central Bus Station

The Tel Aviv New Central Bus Station ("Hatachana Hamerkazit Hachadasha" or simply "Hatachana Hamerkazit") is located at Levinsky 106. It's a huge concrete monster - a surreal, claustrophobic maze of interconnected levels with weird little markets, strange and wonderful stores and confusing signage. If William Gibson and M C Escher had to co-design a futuristic, third world bus station, they couldn't have done it better. Personally, I love it, but some people think of it more like a version of hell. Either way, if you need to catch a bus from here, leave plenty of time. Not only for getting through the queues for the security check at the entrance, but also to find your way around the place and to your desired floor and bay. **Egged** buses leave from levels 6 and 7.

The **Egged information point** is on level 6.

Dan buses leave from level 7. The **Dan information point** is on level 7.

Shared taxis (Moniyot Sheirut) for both Tel Aviv and other cities leave from the car park on Tsemach David St. outside the station building. They are little minivans. The internal Tel Aviv ones are numbered (see below for more info). The intercity ones only leave when they are full, so you may have to wait a while. Signs for intercity destinations are in Hebrew on the front of the taxis, so you may need to ask someone to point out the right taxi or go along and inquire with each driver till you find the one you want. Many of these taxis run on weekends too and they cost the same as the bus.

Rav Kav

Apart from paying cash per ride or buying a day ticket ("hofshi yomi" – good if you're going to take more than two bus rides in a day), Dan buses used to offer multi-ride punch cards that saved you a little bit of money per ride. Those have now all been replaced by Rav Kav, which is a magnetic card you can pre-charge and recharge on buses and at various service points. You can now get one of these cards for 10NIS, then charge it with various amounts or plans. Instead of a punch card, you can charge that amount to your plastic card, saving a little bit of money that way. Ask for an "anonymous card" ("kartis anonnimi") if you don't like the thought of being potentially tracked.

If you're entitled to a discount (such as a student discount) you'll need to register with your picture and ID.

To get a card and register it, you'll need to turn up at one of the service points (see below) with your passport, have your photo taken (for free) and register your details. Useful if you're staying in town for a long time, plan on using the buses regularly and don't mind being spied on by god knows who. Otherwise, you just turn up and get an anonymous card without an ID.

The main service points for issuing Rav Kav cards are:

Central Bus Station, 7th floor (near the Dan info point) * Sun – Thurs 7:00 – 21:00. Fri 7:00 – 13:00

Masof 2000 (by Central Train Station) * Sun – Thurs 8:00 – 20:00, Fri 8:00 – 14:00

There is now also a combined bus and train Rav Kav ticket, which you can get at the Savidor, HaShalom and Tel Aviv University train stations. You will need an ID to get one of those. I am not sure whether it's still possible to get an anonymous one.

Shared Taxis (moniyot sheirut)

These yellow-fronted minibuses follow some bus routes (most importantly the **4** and **5** but note that the no. **5** shared taxi doesn't go all the way to the central train station, but carries on to Ramat Aviv instead) and a ride costs the same as a bus ride. You can't use the **Rav Kav** card on them but apart from that they are much better than the bus and also run on weekends and occasionally late at night. They will pick you up and drop you off anywhere you want along the bus route, not necessarily at bus stops. To stop one, just hail it. If it doesn't stop, it either didn't see you or it's full. Pay when you get on or grab a seat and pass your money down the car to the driver. Your change will be passed back to you. When you want to get off, just tell the driver.

Trains

Most people in Tel Aviv use the trains (http://www.rail.co.il) as means of getting out of town, rather than around town, because the train stations are not particularly central. If you're heading to the University from the more southern parts of town, though, it can be a cheap and fast way of getting there. Trains are regular and comfortable and the journeys can be cheaper than the bus if you're going out of town. There is a combined **Rav Kav** bus & train pass (see above) you can get if you plan on using the train regularly, as well as the buses.

A trip from HaHagana station (about 5 minutes' walk from the central bus station and a short cycle away from, say, Florentin) to the Uni takes around 10-15 minutes. You can take bicycles on trains now at all times apart from rush hour (so basically up to 6:00, from 9:00 – 15:00 and after 19:00). It's free. Look out for the carriages with the signs saying bikes are allowed. Bikes need to be secured to the carriage wall with a strap or a lock. Supposedly station security may ask to see yours before letting you on.

Walking

Tel Aviv's small enough to make it possible to walk everywhere central if that's what you want. Do remember that jaywalking (crossing the road when the little red man is on or crossing not at a zebra crossing when one is nearby) is a crime in Israel. You'll see people doing it all the time, so you may think it's OK, but it isn't according to the law. Occasionally policemen stand by traffic lights and give big spot fines to unsuspecting pedestrians. Officially, cars are meant to stop for you at a zebra crossing, once you put your foot down on the road. In reality...Good luck. Sometimes you just have to insist.

4 Buy food. Eat food.

Supermarkets

AM:PM is the most prominent local chain and you'll see their 24 hour stores everywhere you go. They are expensive and not particularly well-stocked, but are open on weekends and their cashiers are generally lovely. **Tiv Taam in the city** are also pretty common and while no longer 24 hours, are proudly non-Kosher, so you can buy your bacon and ham there if you're keen, as well as bread and other non Passover Kosher stuff during Passover. They are also open on weekends and their prices are often cheaper than AM:PM. A few of their prominent branches are scattered along Dizengoff and Ben Yehuda and there's also a popular one on the corner of Rothschild and Maze. Their green lettering says Tim Taam in Hebrew and "in the city" in English.

Shufersal and **Mega** are the bigger, cheaper supermarkets. There is a big **Shufersal** at 79 Ben Yehuda St. (open till midnight most nights and overnight from Thursday – Friday afternoon) and a big, good **Mega** on the lower ground floor of building A in Dizengoff Center (the **Lev Cinema** one) and on level 3 of the central bus station. These supermarket chains are Kosher, so close early on Friday for the Shabat and reopen Saturday evening. **Victory** on Achad Haam 13 (another branch at Lincoln 16) are even cheaper for many things (including alcohol), although their supermarkets are a tad depressing. The Achad Haam branch is open till 21:00 on weekdays, the Lincoln one till 22:00-23:00.

Markets

Carmel Market (Shuk Hakarmel)
HaKarmel St. (off Allenby Street, parallel to Nahalat Binyamin) *
Sun – Fri daytime, Thurs open late

Tel Aviv's biggest market with lots of cheap fruit and veg, spices, baked goods, sweets, condiments, booze and also non-edibles like clothes and toys. If you do one market in Tel Aviv, do this one, cause it's got everything and is buzzy and exciting. If you're self-catering in any of the main tourist areas, this is where you should be doing your food shopping. Even if you're further away, it's still worth the journey. Not only will you usually beat supermarket prices, but the experience itself will be a thousand times cooler. All the buses that go along Allenby St. stop close to the entrance to the market so you won't have far to walk with your shopping. The quality of the produce in the market is usually very good, but it varies from stall to stall. Go further in for the best deals and it won't hurt to haggle. The best spice and condiment stall in the market is probably the Amrany brothers' which is more or less bang in the centre, on the Western side. You can sometimes get their own brand of olive oil, bottled in recycled mineral water bottles. It's cheap and brilliant. There are a few other spice places, but for the best variety see Levinsky Market below.

At the end of the day (early evenings or late afternoons), especially on Friday afternoons, many stalls will sell off stock cheaply, especially stuff that's a bit off or cosmetically not very nice. You can sometimes even pick up free fruit and veg that's perfectly edible but is not likely to get bought. Handy if you're self catering on a tight budget or are into dumpstering.

Levinsky Market (Shuk Levinsky)

Levinsky Street (between Herzel and HaAliya) and the side streets leading off from it. Most of the action is between Merhavia and HaAliya.* Sun – Thurs till evening, Fri only in the daytime.

Tel Aviv's spice market is actually a stretch of shops offering a mind-blowing explosion of colours, flavours and noises. For me, this is one of those places where Tel Aviv takes off its mask and shows you it really is a part of the Middle East in all its grubby, multicultural glory. The main street is packed with stores selling every kind of spice, herb, nut and seed possible, as well as delis, bakeries, sweetshops and green grocers. **Kaymak** (see Café section) on the corner of Levinsky and Nahalat Binyamin is a great little place to sit and get your bearings. Right next door to the café is **Atlas,** a little spice & herb shop selling (among other things) amazing spice blends for flavouring rice, salads, etc. and freshly ground coffee blends (you can smell them roasting). It's cheap and very well stocked. Up and across the road at no. 46 is the famous **Pereg** spice shop, selling pre-packaged, high quality spices and condiments (so great for taking home with you). Next to Pereg, there is a handy little shop selling oriental cooking ingredients, including tofu and both veggie and non-veggie miso paste. The nearby streets offer all kinds of kitchen and homeware surprises and superb workers' restaurants of all kinds. For the best Persian restaurant in the area, try the tiny but always packed **Salimi**, at Nahlat Binyamin 80. Good if you eat meat, otherwise it's vegetable rice all the way. Across the road at number 91 is a hidden gem of a deli selling excellent cheeses and big blocks of Halva (sesame seed paste sweets). Matalon Street nearby (and spreading onto Herzl) is a candy raver's heaven with lots of wholesalers and retailers selling bizarre toys and flashing gadgetry of all kinds. If that's your kind of thing, carry on to Kefar

Giladi St. for more wholesale shops selling toys, accessories and haberdashery.

Dizengofff Center food market
Dizengoff Center, building B lower ground and ground floor *
Thursday and Friday daytime

Lots of stalls selling freshly prepared food of all kinds to eat there or take away. There's stuff from all over the world including Jewish (of various origins), Thai, Mexican, Italian, Japanese, etc.. Also lots of cakes and other desserts plus the occasional bizarre delicacy. There are also one or two fresh produce stalls, on occasion. It's a good place to grab a tasty, cheap lunch, though it can get very busy and seating is sparse. If you want to make a picnic of it, the nearest park is **Gan Meir** (see **Do Stuff**), about 5 minutes from the shopping centre down King George St.. On a hot day, your food will probably stay warm. The main market day is Friday.

Tel Aviv Port's covered market and farmers' market
http://www.farmersmarket.co.il
http://www.namal.co.il
Tel Aviv Port, in and outside Hanger 12 * Daily apart from Sun 8:00 – 22:00. Farmer's Market outside Thurs – Fri.

Tel Aviv now has a permanent indoor market of quality produce, aiming to be like Borough St. Market in London or Barcelona's La Boqueria (only smaller). It's fun and bright and while not as cheap as the more "common" markets, it's certainly a nice place to visit. It has high quality fruit and veg, breads, cheeses, meats, etc. plus some funky market restaurants and prepared food stalls run by known chefs. Apparently, the building itself is special as it's powered by wind and solar energy. On Thurs - Fri there's also the farmer's market outside - lots of great produce direct from local farmers, plus speciality breads, cakes, flowers and other cool stuff.

For another organic farmers' market on Friday mornings till 15:00, see **Hatachana** in the Shopping section (under Clothes / Areas).

Hatikva Market (Shuk Hatikva)
Entrance is on the corner of Hahagana and Etsel * Bus no. 16
Sun – Thurs early morning – 18:00, Fri early morning – before Shabat

A cool market selling mainly fresh produce – fruit, veg, meat, fish and cheese. Also baked goods and sweets. It's a bit out of the way and the prices are about the same as the more central **Shuk Hakarmel**, so not worth the special journey if you're only looking for a better deal. It's well off the tourist trail, though, so offers a different glimpse into Tel Aviv life and is a fun place to go if you already know the other markets. There are a few good restaurants within the market serving proper Yemenite and Iraqi food. The restaurants on the nearby Etsel Street used to be good but have generally gone downhill in recent years.

Health food stores

Eden Teva Market
http://www.edenteva.co.il (Hebrew only)
Ibn Gabirol 71 (Gan Ha-Ir shopping centre, fountain floor) * 1-800-468-46, Sun – Thurs 8:00 -22:00, Fri 8:00 – 15:00

Part of a big chain and apparently the biggest health food store in Tel Aviv. Spotlessly clean, well-stocked with just about anything imaginable and often relatively cheap, as they have regular special offers.

Teva Kastel

http://www.tevacastel.com/ (Hebrew only)

Israel's biggest chain of organic stores with plenty of shops around Tel Aviv including two on Dizengoff (corner of Frishman and corner of Jabotinsky), Ibn Gabirol 151, Gan Ha-Ir shopping centre (specialist vitamin store) and even in Tel Aviv University.

Nitzat Haduvdevan

Ibn Gabirol 58 * 03-6965174 * Sun – Thur 9:00 – 21:00, Fri 8:00 – 15:00
Shuk haCarmel 30 (Carmel market) * 03-5101497 * Sun – Thur 9:00-18:00, Fri 8:00 – 16:00

Two branches of a smaller chain of stores with a less pristine and more "earthy" feel. Well stocked with a good range of stuff including fresh produce. Prices are relatively low.

Neroli

Shabazi 23 * 03-5107869 * Sun – Thur 8:30 – 20:00, Fri 8:30-16:00

A pretty little independent organic store in the chic Neve Tzedek neighbourhood. Surprisingly well stocked for its small size and offers fresh fruit & veg and even a juice bar.

South Tel Aviv cooperative

http://www.cooptlv.org/ (Hebrew only) * cooperativeta@gmail.com * Tues 18:00 – 20:00, Fri 11:30 – 14:30

Not a shop but a cooperative for bulk buying organic produce directly from the farmers / manufacturers. You can only get stuff from them if you join as a member, so this is only really relevant if you're in town for a while. To join, drop them an email or visit during the opening hours. Joining involves buying a share in the coop for 200NIS. Of this, 150NIS gets returned to you if you decide to leave. They were about to move at the time of writing. Email for current address.

Street food / Fast food

If you wanted to save money, you could easily survive on cheap, filling street food in Tel Aviv. There are places everywhere serving things like falafel, shawarma, pizza, schnitzel, burgers and hummus. You can get a pita full of filling veggie food for less than 20NIS, a bit more for meat, but still not much. There's also now a trend of little sushi bars and healthy fast food. **Note that many street food places only accept cash.** Places are listed below by type.

Some foods I think you should know...

Sabich (the ch is like the ch in Bach, not like the ch in change) is basically the same thing as falafel (with hummus and salads inside a pita) but with fried, sliced aubergine instead of the falafel. It's often served with egg and / or potatoes inside too, so if you're vegan, remember to ask for it without the egg.

Jahnun and **Mallawach** **are** traditional Yemenite fried / cooked filo pastry dishes that are sort of sweet and sort of savoury and a bit heavy (especially the jachnun). They are served with tomato sauce, a spicy sauce called Schug (red or green) and usually an egg. Mallawach is fried, flat and round like a pancake, while the Jacnhnun is more roll shaped and slow cooked.

Burekas is a Turkish filo pastry, usually filled with cheese and / or vegetables. Common fillings are spinach, aubergines, potatoes and mushrooms.

Shakshuka is an egg and tomato breakfast dish, sometimes served with added meat or cheese, but often just with egg, tomatoes and peppers. It's great as a hangover cure and served almost everywhere around town at all hours of the day.

You most likely know what **Hummus** is (mashed chickpeas with tahine sauce, right?), but to prevent any confusion that may arise, here are some other names you should know. **Masabha** and **mashawsha** are slightly different ways of serving the chickpeas: essentially they are served warm and can involve some whole chickpeas rather than all mashed. You can also get **Ful** (like hummus but made of broad beans) that is often mixed with regular hummus to make a far heavier dish that has been compared to having a delicious bowling ball in your stomach. These dishes are usually served with pita bread and pickles on the side. You can sometimes add an egg for a few shekels more (it's worth it, if you're not vegan).

Sahlav (sahlev) / Mallabi are traditional pudding desserts. Sahlev is a sweet hot drink of Turkish origin with a consistency like runny pudding or thick, glossy cream. It's made with powdered orchid roots, hence the name (sahlev means orchid in Turkish and the Hebrew word is sahlav). It's served during the winter months in cafés and also sold at some juice stalls and kiosks. You have it with shredded nuts and cinnamon on top. Mallabi is sort of like semi-clear milk or water-based pudding, served cold with shredded coconut and pistachios and a red berry or rose syrup on top. It's served all year round. The best mallabi in town is also the simplest – no nuts. It's at **Mallabi Djaani** at Sderot Yerushalaim 96 in Jaffa (Sun – Thurs 11:00 – 20:00, Fri 10:00 – 18:00, Saturday 11:00 – 19:30). There's no sign, just a counter and a nice guy. You can buy the powders to make these in the Carmel and Levinsky market.

Make a basic Shakshuka

Ingredients

2 eggs
1-2 cloves of garlic, minced or thinly sliced
2 ripe tomatoes, diced
¼ teaspoon of cumin
Some chili powder to taste or 1 small hot pepper, de-seeded and sliced thinly
Salt & pepper to taste
Some olive oil for frying

Preparation

Heat the oil in a pan, add garlic and cumin and fry for a couple of minutes (beware of burning the garlic). Add tomatoes and chili (or chili pepper) and bring to a boil, cook until tomatoes are soft and make a sort of sauce (you can add a bit of water)

Break eggs into the sauce, without stirring. Cook until done (which depends on how hard you want the eggs to go). Serve with thick sliced of bread or pita bread, which you can use to soak up the sauce.

Variations: add red bell peppers (the original, "official" recipe calls for them), mushrooms or diced aubergine (eggplant) at the beginning (just before the tomatoes) or cheeses (feta, cheddar, etc.) or spinach with the eggs.

Falafel, Hummus and Sabich

Ovad's sabich (Tel Aviv franchise)
Carlibach 18 * Sun – Thur 9:00 – 2:00, Fri 9:00 – 17:00, Sat
20:00 – 3:00

The original branch in nearby town Givatayim serves the self
proclaimed "best sabich in the universe" (and many who've had it
agree, including myself). This branch, while lacking in Ovad
himself – a somewhat quirky character with a serving routine
worthy of a standup comedian – does serve exceedingly good
sabich, served by staff who've all undergone rigorous training
with the master himself.

Falafel Frishman and Sabich Frishman
The corner of Frishman and Dizengoff. Sun – Thurs 10:00 –
00:00, Fri 10:00 – Shabat, Sat end of Shabat – 00:00

Two little places side by side, one serves falafel and the other
sabich in either a regular or a whole-wheat pita. They've been
there for god knows how many years and are still serving the
best sabich in town as far as I'm concerned. The falafel is good
too, by all accounts. For a slightly different taste, try the "cheese
sabich", made with feta cheese instead of (or with) hummus.
They also sell beer.

Falafel Hippo
Ibn Gabirol 64 * Sun – Thurs 11:00 – 24:00, Fri 11:00 – Shabat,
Sat Shabat – 24:00
Dizengoff 70 * Sun – Thurs 10:00 – 22:00, Fri 10:00 – 16:00

Yummy organic falafel, sabich, hummus and salads without the
inflated price tag you'd usually associate with organic food.

Served with a regular or whole-wheat pita and there are even gluten free options.

Hakosem
Shlomo Hamelech 1 * 03-5252033 * Sun – Thurs 9:30 – 23:00

This hugely popular place is the perfect one stop shop for everything that's good about local street food, from falafel and sabich to shawarma (donner), shakshuka and hummus. Service is fast and everything is yummy.

Abu Dubby
King George 81 * Sun – Thurs 10:00 – 21:00, Fri 10:00 – 19:00, Sat 10:00 – 20:00

This place is easy to find as it's decorated in the colours of the Jamaican flag. Apart from decent hummus and good vibrations, you can get a dose of tasty reggae, dub and roots music. You can also get a free refill for your hummus and free coffee at the end (to have with a non-free baklava, if you so wish). They also run a reggae music label, so you can buy some cheap CDs by local artists knowing all proceeds go to the artists themselves, as well as tickets to various gigs and parties (not just reggae).

Abu Hassan's
Shivtei Israel 14, Jaffa * 03-6828355
Sun - Fri 8:00 – 15:00
(another kiosk-like branch at haDolphin 1, Jaffa)

Merkaz hahummus ha'asli (the pedigree hummus centre)
Yefet 73, Jaffa * Phone: 03-6813435
Sun – Sat 7:00 – 21:00 (times are approximate)

Everyone in Tel Aviv agrees that for the best hummus in the area, you need to go to Jaffa. Every Friday, half of Tel Aviv does just that and you can see the traffic gridlocked in Kikar HaShaon ("the clock square") as people make their way to their usual place. Which place serves the best hummus in Jaffa is a matter of great debate. Everyone has a favourite place that they swear by to the exclusion of all others. The places above are both famous and extremely popular so avoid going on Friday lunchtime if you want to be seated in a hurry (or at all). **Abu Hassan's** is closer to the flea market area and Tel Aviv and is bigger and somewhat posher looking (though by no means posh). It's the most popular of the lot and serves only hummus-based dishes. Their hummus is superb. **Merkaz Hahummus** is further into Jaffa proper and also has a devoted following, including my dad, who refused to eat hummus anywhere else. It has two spaces across the road from each other and the waiters will often run across the road to move stuff from one side to the other. Apart from hummus it also serves falafel, various salads and meat dishes.

Mashawsha
Pinsker 40 (corner of Bograshov) * 03-6293796
Sun – Thurs 11:00 – 23:00, Fri till 17:00, Sat 12:00-23:00

A pleasant place to sit in the Bograshov area and have a Galilee-style hummus dish. Gets very busy on weekends.

Burekas

Burekas Amikam
Ibn Gabirol 21 * 03-6204728
Sun – Thurs 24 hours, Fri 6:00 – Shabat, Sat end of Shabat – 2:00

This is a very well known place that gets very busy. They serve various kinds of cheese Burekas (plain or with olives, spinach, etc.) plus a mushroom and potato one. If you want to eat in you can sit at the counter.

Burekas Penso
Levinsky 43 * Sun – Thurs 6:00 – 20:00, Fri 6:00 – 16:00

A family owned place selling decent Burekas, though a tad oily. You can also buy pita bread, Turkish bread and other baked goodies. In winter they sell Sahlev. There are a few seats inside.

Burekas Mis
Stern 5 * Sun – Thurs 6:30 – 19:30, Fri 6:30 – 16:30

Florentin's cheap and decent neighbourhood bakery selling proper Burekas (egg and all), plus various cookies, cakes, mini-pizzas, etc. Mostly self service from big tins and piles.

Lilach Deli
Sderot Yerudhalaim 83 (corner of Dante), Jaffa * 03-6838788 * Sun – Thurs 9:00 – 20:00, Fri 9:00 – 16:30

Come early for what has been referred to as the best burekas in Jaffa and possibly elsewhere. They also serve various home made Balkan dishes, stews, etc..

***

There is also an old man on the corner of the Carmel Market and Raban Gamliel 28 that makes a mean Turkish Burekas sandwich Sun – Thur from around 9:00-13:00.

Pizza

Tony Vespa
Rothschild 140 * 03 – 5460000 Sun – Sat 12:00 – 3:00
Dizengoff 267 * 03 – 5460000 Sun – Sat 18:00 – 0:200

Not Kosher. Gourmet, thin-crust pizza sold by the weight. The slices are not triangular but are cut into rectangles and are then weighed. The ingredients are all natural with an emphasis on freshness and the pizza is very light. There are lots of creative toppings to choose from that will please meat eaters and veggies alike: bacon is a popular one and there are plenty of interesting cheese and vegetable combinations, some unique to this place.

Giuseppe
Vital 3 * 0545928244 Sun – Sat 18:00 till about 1:00. Closed Fridays.

Cash only. Florentin's family run neighbourhood pizza place where all the true locals hang out. Knowledge of this place is passed from person to person so I will probably get killed now for having broken the first rule of Pizza Club. You can watch them make their excellent, thin-crust pizza behind the little counter while you wait in the queue, as the place is always busy, especially late at night. The menu is basic and is on the wall, in Hebrew. It's Kosher dairy so your choices are different kinds of veg, cheeses and fish (tuna and anchovies). If you're in a hurry order whatever (huge) slices they have ready on the counter or you may have to wait 15 minutes or more for your pizza. People will cut in line if you're too slow, so think fast. It's worth asking if there's anything about to come out of the oven and stake your claim to some of that, if you want to stay a step ahead of the competition.

Pizza Bazilikum, just south of the corner of Abarbanel and Florentin provides a lesser alternative for when Giuseppe is shut. It has a good party vibe and great music but the pizza isn't that great. **Habarbanel,** more or less across the road from the **Hoodna** (see Bars section) sells the cheapest pizza in Florentin and also has a cheap bar upstairs.

Il Pizzaiolo
Ben Yehuda 122 * 03-5239846 * Sun – Thurs – 12:00 – 00:30, Fri 12:00 – hour before Shabbat, Sat an hour after Shabbat – 00:30

Right next door to the excellent **Dolce Melody** (see in Ice Cream places below) is this unassuming place with surprisingly excellent thin crust pizza. It's Kosher, so no meat, but there are plenty of choices to keep anyone happy. Beautiful, beautiful pizza in the heart of the Ben Yehuda French tourist area.

***

See more Italian places in the **Eat out. Drink out** section.

Asian

Dim Sum Station
Yehuda Halevi 44 (near corner with Nahalat Binyamin) 077-2344954 * Sun – Wed 11:00 – 22:00, Thurs 11:00 – 23:00, Fri 11:00- 16:00, Sat 11:00 – 00:00

Not Kosher. A tiny place with only two small bars for seating. They serve excellent, cheap dim sum with plenty of meaty, shrimpy and veggie options. They also serve noodles, soups and stews.

Salaam Bombay
Allenby 124 * Sun – Thurs 12:00 – 18:00

A worker style Indian restaurant with cheap meat and veggie dishes. Very simple looking but the food is good, as is the chai.

Hasushia
Rothschild 45 * Sun – Wed 11:30 – 1:00, Thurs, Fri 11:30 – 2:00, Sat 12:30 – 2:00
Ben Yehuda 77 * Sun – Wed 11:30 – 1:00, Thurs, Fri 11:30 – 2:00, Sat 12:30 – 1:00
Ibn Gavirol 54 * Sun – Wed 11:30 – 2:00, Thurs, Fri 11:30 – 3:00, Sat 12:30 – 2:00

A popular chain of sushi places. Fast food style, eat in or takeaway, plus they also do deliveries (*9969 from any Israeli phone). It's far from gourmet but edible enough. Plenty of veggie options. **Not Kosher.**

Health Food/ veggie / vegan

For the best healthy vegan takeaway place in Tel Aviv, try **Buddha Burgers** in the restaurant section.

Fresh kitchen
http://www.freshkitchen.co.il (Hebrew only)
Ben yehuda 77 * 03-5292687 * Sun – Thurs 11:30 – 00:00, Fri 12:00 – 17:00
New branch at Dizengoff 149 and there are also branches at Basel 37 and on Yehuda HaMaccabi.

Consciously healthy food cafés with lots of nutritionally balanced options for meat eaters, veggies and vegans - café style eat in or takeaway. They also do gluten-free dishes, though those are predominantly salads, making me think they are as much about bandwagon-hopping than anything else.

The veggie Shwarma (Hashawarma Hatzimchonit)
King George 81 * 03-5248821 * 12:00 – 00:00 daily

Next door to the popular Abu Dubby humus place is this 100% vegan fastfood place serving burgers, wraps, salads, patties and, of course, shwarma (donner kebab / giro). It's still new and getting very popular so service can be a bit random, especially when it's busy. Still, the food is tasty, mostly based on tofu/seitan, though the patties are made out of lentils, I believe. There's another branch in Florentin, on Washington Blvd.

Malawah and Jahnun

Hummus Habayit (formerly Hajahnun shel Ima)
Allenby 47 * Sun – Thur 10:00 – 22:00, Fri 9:00 – 24:00, Sat 12:00 – 22:00.

A small, friendly place serving fine malawah and jahnun, plus chulnt (a traditional crockpot dish with meat, potatoes, beans, etc.) on Fridays. It now offers other things too like shakshuka (including a vegan one) and hummus dishes. The food is traditional, but unlike the usual, Kosher jahnun places, this place is open on weekends and is a fun place to have a cool late night snack.

Bakeries, patisseries, sandwiches

Tel Aviv's full of good bakeries, serving up tasty bread, delicious cakes and other baked lovelies. Sugar and gluten free options are becoming increasingly popular.

A standard patisserie (or any bakery that specialises in cake and sweets) is called a "kondituria" (or "konditoria") in Israel. Any place that calls itself a patisserie is likely to be more upmarket and / or pretentious and therefore more expensive.

Kurtosh
Lincoln 18 * 07-78280606 Sun – Thurs 7:00 – 24:00, Fri 7:00 – Shabat
Bograshov 39 * 03-5280606 Sun – Thurs 7:00 – 21:00, Fri 7:00 – Shabat
Dizengoff 178 * 03-5273434 Sun – Thurs 8:00 – 24:00, Fri 8:00 – Shabat, Sat: An hour after end of Shabat – 24:00

A Hungarian bakery / café specialising in an odd but gloriously delicious tubular yeast cake-like pastry called, perhaps unsurprisingly, a kurtosh (which the locals pronounce "kyortush"). You can watch it being made on big metal tubes at any of their branches and choose from a range of toppings and fillings, some traditional, some less so. It's one of the best cake things you're likely to experience in Tel Aviv and big, too – easily enough for several people. They also serve other types of cake (including some good sugar-free options) and hot drinks. The Bograshov and Dizengoff branches are pretty small with limited seating. The Lincoln branch is a bit bigger, but sort of out of the way, unless you hit it late on your way out clubbing. There's now another branch in the Jaffa flea market, on Olei Tsion St.

Kondituria Weiss
King George 7 * 03-5285421 * Sun – Thurs 7:00 – 20:00, Fri
7:00 – 15:00

They make the best poppy seed cake this side of anywhere. It's
not cheap but it's very much worth it. You can now get it in
individual slices too. Apart from that, they do a good selection of
other sweet baked goods, as well as burekas and other savoury
treats.

Abulafia
Yefet 7, Jaffa
Herbert Samuel 54 (Tayelet / seafront) * hours: 24/7

This place is owned by a very well respected Arab family from
Jaffa and has been around since 1879. It's not the best bakery by
any means, but it's there when you need it and good for killing
your appetite and avoiding the extortionate prices of the beach
cafés. Don't expect anything but thick, heavy dough, though.

Dievuchka
Hahalutsim 41 * Sun – Fri 8:00 – 17:00 * 050-7416217

Not quite a bakery, but a beautiful gourmet sandwich place /
café. Their sandwiches are divine and meticulously made and
there's also soup and, occasionally, stews. One of the contenders
for best sandwiches in town.

For a more traditional Florentin sandwich try the deli at **Frenkel
28**. It's run by a couple well into their 80s and is very old school.
Their smoked fish sandwiches are said to be the best in town.

Yahaloma
Zevulun 5 * Sun-Froi 8:30-17:30

A real hidden gem of a similar style to the above: part deli, part tiny market bistro, this pretty little place serves beautifully presented and yummy sandwiches, stews, salads and other innovative dishes drawing on local cuisine and ingredients. Everything comes with good coffee and friendly service.

Lachmanina
Yona Kremnitski 14 * 03-7448088 * Sun – Thur 7:00 -20:00, Fri 7:00 – 17:00

One of Tel Aviv's true hidden treasures, this lovely bakery/café is owned by a couple of women with a truly amazing life story (read about it here - http://bit.ly/wtOlOb). It started as a home business and has grown into a cool café serving excellent sandwiches and cakes that are all hand made. Their products are not cheap, but absolutely legendary, especially things like the Nelson bread (stuffed full of all kinds of wholesome seeds and things) You can also buy other unique products here like wine, jams and olive oil, all made by family and friends. This place is certainly off the tourist trail, but is only about 15 minutes' walk from the Azrieli centre, in a sweet residential neighbourhood.

Itzik and Ruthie
Sheinkin 53 * 03 – 6852753 * Sun – Fri 4:00 – 15:00

This place has been around for over 50 years and serves legendary sandwiches, shakshukas and more, all perfect for late night munchies or early riser cravings. Try the Shakshuka in a bun, a bargain at 18NIS or the "gazoz" (soda pop). The opening hours listed are not wrong – they really do open at 4AM.

Margoza Bakery
Margoza 24, Jaffa * 03-6817787
Sun – Thurs 7:00 – 19:00, Fri 7:00 – 16:00

Make no mistake – this pretty, friendly little bakery / café is definitely one of the signs of the unavoidable gentrification of the flea market area of Jaffa. Their stuff is so good, though, I'm willing to forgive and forget. They sell various speciality breads, cakes, biscuits and other desserts and also serve hot drinks. It's a nice place to sit and enjoy a freshly baked brioche, unless you hit yummy mommy hour when the place becomes overrun with screaming toddlers.

Piece of cake
Yehuda Hayamit 17, Jaffa * Sun – Thurs 7:00 – 20:00, Fri 7:00-17:00 / There's now another branch at 46 King George St.

A huge choice of bread, cakes, burekas, etc. made with love, including a good selection of sugar and gluten free stuff. This place practically has a cult following. They also run **Café Alma** across the road (next door to **Abu Hassan's** hummus), which is surprisingly posh-looking for the area.

I love Cupcakes
http://www.ilovecupcakes.co.il
Ben Yehuda 114 * 03- 5222243 * Sun – Thurs 09:00-21:00, Fri 09:00 – 17:00,

Israel's first dedicated cupcake store is beautiful and chic. Apart from cupcakes, you can also buy flowers and sparkling wine, making it every girl's Sex and the City dream.

Mutran Sweets
Yefet 99, Jaffa * 03-6574527 * 9:00 – 1:00 daily

Traditional Arab sweets from the famous family from Nazareth. They produce and import some of the best in the business and are well aware of it. It's well worth the trip, but is not cheap.

Coffee, tea, spices and sweets

The best place in town for spices, herbal tea infusions and exotic drink mixes is the **Levinsky Market** listed above. You can also buy pretty good blends of freshly ground coffee there. Jaffa has some good coffee places too. You can try **Café Paul** (see **Eat out. Drink out** chapter) for some very high quality blends, or see below for more options.

Tiran Spices
http://tiran-spices.co.il (Hebrew only)* Yefet 121, Jaffa * 03-6588045

A family business specialising in exotic coffee blends, Middle Eastern sweets (including amazing Syrian Halva), herbs & spices. Some of their coffee blends are unique to them and very highly regarded. They're the biggest sellers of Arabic coffee in Jaffa and are basically a whole spice market stuffed into one store.

Café Vemamtakim (Coffee and Candy)
Allenby 107 * 03-5663063

As the name suggests, this unassuming little store specialises in freshly ground coffee, imported blends and other teas and exotic drinks from around the world (including Yerba Mate). There's also a huge range of chocolates and international sweets.

Coffee Lab

Carmel 21 * 03-5104121 * Sun – Thur 8:30 – 18:30, Fri 7:30 – 17:30

A little coffee shop / store for aficionados tucked away in the Carmel Market. It sells over 38 varieties of coffee you can take away with you, though makes a fine stop if you need a quick espresso fix, too.

Palais Des Thes

http://www.palaisdesthes.co.il
Dizengoff 131 (Corner of Gordon) * 03-5221317 * Sun – Thur 9:30 – 20:00, Fri 9:00 – 15:00

A posh and beautiful tea store / tea house, specialising in international teas, tea gifts, tea pots and tea related stuff.

Beatrice

Rashi 19 (corner of King George 22) * 03-5256415 * Sun – Thurs 10:00 – 20:00, Fri 9:00 – 16:00

This super sweet Dutch deli is where you want to be for everything you know and love from the Netherlands. There's a huge selection of sweet things, but also cheeses, wine, pickles, condiments and even smoked fish. Their chocolate range extends further into Europe.

Alcohol

Buying alcohol in Tel Aviv isn't hard – practically everywhere sells it. If you want specialist alcohol places with good deals on booze, though, see below.

Local brews

Israel has an increasing number of excellent microbreweries that make great beers from blondes to stouts. Among them are Shapira, Malka, Bazelet (comes from the Golan Heights), Golda, Negev and many more. There is also good Palestinian beer – Taybe beer. Some are available in some cafés, supermarkets and bars around town, but some are only available in specialist alcohol stores so keep an eye out for them.

HaAliya Street

Head south from where Allenby meets HaAliya for a row of cheap alcohol stores with frequent special offers on local and imported beers, spirits and wine. It's best to try a few and check the prices as prices can vary widely based on what deals they happen to have on.

Hinawy's (Wine and more)
Nahum Goldman 8 * 03-6831538 * Sun – Thur 9:00 – 21:00, Fri-Sat 8:00 – 20:00
Carlibach 25 * 03-6240458 * Sun – Thur 9:00 – 21:00, Fri 9:00 – 17:00

Ben Yehuda 224 * 03-7366461 * Sun – Wed 9:00 -21:00 (Thur 22:00), Fri 8:00-17:00, Sat 12:00 – 19:00

A chain of big stores with a huge choice of reasonably priced booze, including a good selection of local and imported boutique beers. It's one of the few places in town that sells the Palestinian Taybe beer. The Carlibach and Ben Yehuda branches also have impressive delis selling cheese, meats, olive oil and loads of other excellent stuff.

Beer Market
Carmel market, corner of Carmel St. and Rambam * open during market hours

A modern new stall selling only Israeli boutique beers and staffed by local experts on the subject. Great for stocking up on local beers to take home, or even sit at the bar and have a beer as part of your market experience.

Ice cream

Even winter in Tel Aviv doesn't feel like winter most of the time, so ice cream places flourish all year round. When things start to heat up for summer, they usually bring out all kinds of really imaginative ice cream flavours, some of which you're not likely to get anywhere else in the world. In winter, they often branch out into serving a wider range of hot drinks, Belgian waffles and hot desserts.

To be honest, there are plenty of good ice cream places around and they're pretty much all good and full of innovative flavours. Here are some of the most popular ones.

Glida Sicilianit (Sicilian ice cream)
Ben Yehuda 110 * Sun – Sat 12:00 – 1:00
Ivn Gvirol 63 * Sun – Thurs 11:00 – 24:00, Fri – Sat 11:00 – last customer

This is probably the best place in Tel Aviv for chocolate lovers: they do a 70% cocoa dark chocolate flavour that is a bit of a local legend and about 4 or 5 other gorgeous chocolate varieties. They also have a very good range of soya ice cream for the vegan and lactose intolerant. It's sweetened with fructose, so is also suitable for some diabetics. The Ben Yehuda branch is the prettier of the two and is next door to a branch of **Iceberg**, another popular chain which also has a huge selection of very exciting flavours, although they are certainly the most sugary of the gourmet bunch. Try their kulfi ice cream and their amazing alcoholic sorbets. Diabetics will find a few good sugar-free flavours.

Dolce Melody
Ben Yehuda 122 * Sun – Sat 9:00 – 1:00

The original Italian ice cream on Ben Yehuda Street, located next door to a great pizza place (see above in pizzas), so you can pretend you're actually in Italy. Their ice cream has the perfect texture and the perfect level of sweetness. They also have a good range of diet, fat free ice cream and sorbets.

Vaniglia
Bograshov 33 * 11:00 – 00:00 daily
Ibn Gavirol 98 * 11:00 – 1:00 daily
Hatachana shopping area * 11:00 – 00:00 daily
Yirmiyahu 23 (corner of Dizengoff) 11:00-1:30 daily

This chain is known for very adventurous ice cream flavours, served alongside the more familiar ones. Expect the unexpected as new flavours are introduced each season. How about celery sorbet or creamy basil ice cream?

Shaked
Hangar 7, Tel Aviv port * 7:00 – 1:00 daily

This place serves café food and fresh juices as well, but is mostly known for its unique ice cream. There are many seasonal flavours, including alcoholic ice cream and things like redbull ice cream, limoncello sorbet and other surprises popular with Israeli clubbers who frequent the port.

If you're in the port area, you may also want to check out **Glida Montana** at building (not hangar) 37 by the port entrance closest to Dizengoff St., which was Tel Aviv's most happening ice cream place in the 60s and 70s. It's still in the same old building (now crumbling) run by the same old guys serving nothing but soft serve vanilla ice cream which you can get topped up with either chocolate or berry sauce. Great if you like faded seaside nostalgia, otherwise it can be a bit depressing.

Capitolina
Olei Zion 9, Jaffa * 03-6036275 * 11:00 – 1:00 daily

Award winning, amazing boutique ice cream made with natural ingredients and love. Lots of amazing flavours including great tasting sugar free options.

Juice Bars

Tel Aviv's full of great juice bars serving fruit and veg juice and occasionally other drinks and even food. Even the most basic ones will serve orange and carrot, plus pomegranate in season (autumn – spring). The better-stocked ones will serve practically every fresh fruit / veg combination imaginable but are likely to be more expensive.

Good ones are:

The one on Sheinkin Street, just up the hill from the corner with Feierberg: staffed predominantly by hot guys who make great soups in winter and know their way around a fruit cocktail. You can also get some lovely little cakes here and chill playing backgammon

The one in the Carmel market, on the corner with Rambam Street: the lovely lady who runs the place will tell you all about the nutrients in your juice and how best to absorb them (a drop or two of olive oil in your juice), plus her prices are low. **Tamara** on the corner of Dizengoff and Ben Gurion is open 24 hours.

5 Eat Out. Drink Out

In a city where cafés usually serve booze and stay open till well past midnight, bars serve gourmet meals and takeaway pizza places sell beer, the lines between cafés, bars and restaurants are generally kinda blurry. It's rare to find a place that isn't a bar-café, a café-restaurant or a bar-restaurant. Usually they are a combination of all three, apart from dance bars that are distinctly bar or even club-like. I've divided up best I can, but basically, if you're looking for somewhere to go that involves the consumption of food and drink, look in all three sections below. Also, if you're looking for a patisserie-type café (the European kind that's open in the day and serves coffee, tea and cake only), pizza and fast food places, I've listed some more of those in the appropriate sections of the **Buy Food** chapter.

Many bars stay open "until last customer", which usually means around 3-4AM when the bar staff get tired and kick you out. Remember that many of the 24 hour cafés sell booze around the clock too (beer at the very least), so you can always move to one of those.

I'm sure you'll notice that my restaurant guide includes lots of stuff about vegan and vegetarian restaurants. This is because I'm a vegetarian. If you're into meat: don't worry. Israelis love their meat and Tel Aviv is full of burger joints, meaty restaurants and even fast food steak places. Most of the places I mention do serve good meat and seafood dishes, in fact, some specialise in both.

In regards to tipping, waiters expect around 15% or so and tipping is expected even if the service was shit, which it often is. You can get away with tipping 12%, especially if you only had coffee at a café. Bar staff expect to be similarly tipped if you're sat at the bar for any significant length of time. Occasionally, bar staff expect you to tip them per drink order (12-15%) even if you're sitting somewhere else and are just picking up your drinks. This is usually the case in the more commercial places, but is becoming increasingly common elsewhere too. Similarly to the States, it pays to tip well at the beginning of the evening if you're sat at the bar. If the bar staff like you, you'll sometimes get free booze.

For information about smoking in restaurants, bars and cafés in Tel Aviv, see the **Useful Info** section.

Restaurants

Hot Spots

These places are not necessarily underground but are trendy, cool and popular with local creatives, media professionals and (occasionally) yuppies. They're great for a nice meal somewhere special and distinctive. The food is super good, the design is stylish and the prices are generally on the higher end of the scale. You should probably book a table when you go. None of these are Kosher.

Joz Veloz
Yehuda Halevi 51 (entrance is down the side of the building) *
03-5606385 * Sun – Fri 12:00 – 1:00

Modern Israeli Italian fusion. This gourmet shabby-chic place
is underground for "grown ups" – very much informal Tel Aviv
style but upmarket with it. It's very popular with local media
darlings and is a bit of a badly kept secret, hidden away in a less
than scenic street but always busy. Everything here is designed
to be quirky and cool, from the perfectly mismatched retro
furniture to the menus – printed daily on an old-style typewriter
(in Hebrew only, but the waitresses speak excellent English). The
food is superb, but quite expensive (around 90NIS for some
mains is not unheard of) and the dishes are often European sized
– much smaller than the average Israeli dish. The place is a bit
pretentious, but it does it so well it actually makes for a very
pretty and unusual place to have a romantic or friendly meal. The
same lesbian couple that owns this place owns a cool bar-café
place too. See **Bata & Gariga** in the bar section.

Tsfon Abraxas (Abraxas North)
Lilienblum 40 * 03-5166660 * Sun 18:00 – 4:00, Mon – Thurs
12:00 – 4:00, Fri-Sat 13:00 – 4:00

Crazy Israeli fusion. This great place is run by a famous and
very quirky local TV chef and is a bit of an experience. There's a
menu that changes daily and a funky design (piles of fresh veg
are an integral part of the décor). The excellent, often spicy food
has plenty of meat, seafood and veggie stuff with innovative
takes on local dishes, including things like pita bread filled with
shrimps or beetroot carpaccio. The food is meant for sharing,
often with your hands and off paper placemats, as there are no
individual plates, just those the dishes are served in. Service is
friendly but casual in typical Israeli style. This place is not cheap

(wine is especially costly) but totally worth it for a good meal and the unusual, uniquely Tel Aviv vibe.

Nanuchka
Lilienblum 30 * 03-5162254 * 12:00 – last customer daily

Georgian. A cheerful, trendy lounge bar / restaurant with colourful quirky décor, a good selection of cocktails and authentic Georgian food. It has a party atmosphere almost every day of the week and there's even a little dance floor. Booking is recommended if you want to eat, especially on weekends.

Brasserie
Ibn Gabirol 77 * 03-6966123 * 24 hours daily

24 hours. A very trendy place popular with local celebrities and affluent professionals. Part French bistro, part upmarket New York City diner, it has a swish, modern design, good food and a great late night menu for dinner (or breakfast) between 1:00-7:00.

Delicatessen
http://delitlv.co.il/
Yehuda Halevi 79/81 * 03-9681010 * Sun – Thur 7:30-20:00, Fri 7:30 – 17:00, Sat 8:00 – 18:00

Various. Business lunch heaven (or hell, depending on who you ask), this place is certainly bourgeois, but bright, airy and very pleasant. It's buzzy and busy with sharp professionals, rich middle aged ladies and local media personalities and the food is good, though not cheap. The menu changes daily and includes a choice of cuisines from Middle Eastern and Mediterranean to East European, American and Asian, all served with a smile. Downstairs you can buy cheaper takeaway dishes, cakes, coffee or juice and sit outside at one of the little tables set up on the pavement. You can also buy excellent conserves, olive oil, cheese, etc..

Hotel Montefiore
http://www.hotelmontefiore.co.il/restaurant.html
Montefiore 36 * 03-5646100 * 7:00 – 24:00 daily

You might not be able to afford to stay at this beautiful, ultra expensive boutique hotel, but if you're after some upmarket European charm, the chic restaurant/ bar at the hotel lobby is worth a visit and is actually quite reasonably priced. The cuisine is predominantly French with some local and Vietnamese touches, the portions are good sized and the service is excellent. The "business lunch", served Sun-Thurs 12:00 – 17:00 is a very good deal and the breakfast is really nice and can be accompanied by some fine morning cocktails.

Container
http://www.container.org.il
Old Jaffa Port, by the boats and the water's edge * 03-6836321 * Sun – Thur 12:00 – late, Fri-Sat, 10:00-late

This is a trendy place in a beautiful location overlooking Jaffa's active fishing port and the sea. It's a restaurant (specialising in seafood, but with options for meat lovers and veggies as well), as well as a bar, an art space and a music venue. There are regular free gigs here by some of Israel's best alternative musicians in genres extending from indie rock to gypsy, Middle Eastern and even some electronica. Weekend brunch and summer sunsets are particularly popular. Recent celebrity sightings at this place included U2's own Bono, who was on a personal visit to Israel, so you never know who you might see here.

Haachim

Ibn Gabirol 12 * 03-6917171 * 12:00-00:00 daily, later on Mondays & Thursdays.

A fun, trendy take on traditional local kebab and shwarma eateries, this cool place serves gourmet versions of both meat and veggie local dishes and prices are restaurant-grade, but not overly expensive. It has a young, party atmosphere. Good local DJs play on Mon and Thur nights and the place usually has mad street parties on holidays such as Purim and Independence Day.

Benedict

Rothschild 29 * 03-6868657 * 24 hours
Ben Yehuda 171 * 03-5440345 * 24 hours

24 hours. Tel Aviv being a non-stop city, a 24 hour breakfast place had to be invented sooner or later and this is it. This chain isn't exactly as trendy as the other places I've written about here, but is hugely popular nonetheless. It's the place to go if you fancy a full English at 2AM or huevos rancheros for lunch. There are plenty of veggie options too, though a not so much on the vegan front. The branch on Rothschild feels more like a yuppie diner and the Ben Yehuda branch is more like a pleasant neighbourhood café. Neither are cheap, but you get a lot for your money.

Cheap and cheerful local flavours

These places are casual, unpretentious and often simple in style, bordering, sometimes, on street food or fast food joints. Prices are generally low.

Gedera 26
Gedera 26 (corner of Hilel Hazaken) * 03-5100164 * Sun – Thurs 12:00 – 17:00 and 19:00 – last customer, Fri 11:00 – 16:00

Swedish, Moroccan and Israeli fusion. This place is the missing link between the hot spots and the cheap places. It's my favourite of the chef-run "market restaurants" in town - a small, bright, unpretentious place that serves yummy, reasonably priced food that tastes like it's been lovingly home cooked by someone who knows what they're doing. The menu changes regularly and offers veggie, fish and meat dishes, all beautifully presented and freshly made with ingredients from the nearby Carmel market. Service is friendly but not always fast. The outside seating is great for people watching. The dinner menu is more expensive and the vibe is a bit less fast paced so good for a romantic dinner.

Hamiznon
Ibn Gabirol 23 * 03-7168977 * Sun – Fri 12:00 – 2:00, Sat 18:00 – 2:00 * Newer branch at king George 30.

Crazy Israeli fast food fusion. This place could have easily gone into the **Buy Food. Eat food** section, as it's essentially a glorified fast food place where the vast majority of dishes are served in pita bread. However, the fact that it's owned by the same chef as **Tsfon Abraxas** means the food, while pricier than your average street food meal, is among the tastiest in town.

Meat, seafood and veggie dishes are on offer, loosely based on popular local dishes but with unique and refreshing twists. Everything is of superior quality, including the pita bread itself. Great for sampling the chef's talents if you can't afford a full blown meal at **Tsfon Abraxas**, as this place is still cheaper than a proper restaurant. My favourite dish here is the potato in a pita. Hard to believe, but it's gorgeous. The King George branch does an ice cream in a pita dish.

Shmaiya
Vital 2 * Sun – Thurs 11:00 – 20:00, Fri till 16:00

Home cooked Israeli fusion. Another one of Florentin's little secrets, this simple place serves cheap meaty and veggie home cooked meals and hummus until the food runs out (the hummus runs out at lunchtime). When the food is cooking, the whole street smells absolutely gorgeous and people come from far and wide to taste the stews, stuffed veg, meat balls and salads, all delicious.

Hamitbachon
Rabbi Akiva 18 (corner of Gedera) * 03-5163689 * 8:00 – 3:00 daily

Home cooked Israeli / Mediterranean. A very casual, cheap and cheerful place serving a good selection of local foods. Don't expect gourmet dining, but this is very much the real Tel Aviv as experienced by many its local workers and slackers, young and old.

Shakshukan

Moshe Hess 4 * 03-6295128 * Sun – Thurs 10:00 – 22:00, Fri 9:00-17:00, Sat 10:00 – 16:00

A cute bistro-style place specialising in shakshuka. They have a changing menu with 13 different variations of the dish (see the **Buy Food. Get Food** chapter for more information about it), including some meaty versions. The coolest twist, though, is that the shaksuka is served in a bread bowl. They also serve other dishes apart from shaksuka, in case you're wondering.

HaTarnegol

http://www.hatarnegol.com (Hebrew only)
Sheerit Israel 4, Jaffa * 037444332 * hatarnegol@hatarnegol.com
* Sun – Wed 8:00 – 17:00, Thur 8:00 – 00:00, Fri 9:00 – 17:00

A small "workers' chef restaurant", serving tasty versions of popular local dishes and innovative derivatives at reasonable prices. It's certainly off the beaten track (unless you're in Jaffa), but worth the trip for the fun vibe, good food and various events they host, from indie film showings to poetry nights, live music and more.

Abu El Abed

Yefet 92, Jaffa * 03-6814665 * 8:00 – 23:00 daily

Middle Eastern. This place has been around since 1949 and still serves super authentic and excellent Arabic/Palestinian food at conveniently cheap prices. The fried cauliflower here is legendary and is in itself worth the trip down to Jaffa.

Hazaken veHayam (the old man and the sea)
Kedem 83, Jaffa * 03-6818699 * 11:00-1:00 daily

Middle Eastern/Fish. A huge, long established, family run restaurant with a big sea-facing terrace. The food is cheap, tasty and there's loads of it, including loads of excellent free salads, included in the price of the main dish. Although the restaurant specialises in fish, vegetarians/vegans will be able to make a meal of the salads, while meat eaters won't feel hard done by either. Come if you're ready to seriously eat. Great for big groups.

Hateimani (The Yemenite)
Yehuda Halevi 29 * Sun – Thur 10:00 – 18:00, Fri 10:00 – 15:00

This small, simple place is one of my favourite discoveries and serves amazing hummus and slow-cooked soup and stew type dishes (both meat and veggie/vegan) at impossibly low prices. A filling and tasty rice and beans dish costs only 12NIS to take away!

See the **Buy food. Eat Food** section for more cheap and cheerful fast food / street food places.

Italian

Pronto
Herzl 4 * 03-5660915 * Sun – Thur 12:30 – 1:00, Fri-Sat 12:30 – 2:00

Not Kosher. One of Tel Aviv's most famous Italian restaurants and considered one of the best in Israel, this upmarket yet relaxed place was previously on Nachmani St.. It has reopened in new, larger premises with an updated menu and an attractive modern design. It's not cheap but great for a special meal.

Pappa's
Hillel Hazaken 12 * 03-5108787
Sun – Sat 12:00 – 1:00

Not Kosher. The food here is good and the setting is really lovely – a beautifully restored old building with retro lamps and fans hanging off the high ceilings. Add to that the soundtrack which is full of jazzy oldies and romantic Italiana and you may well feel like you've been whisked away to a 30s B&W movie about pizza. Even with the neat décor, the place manages to be relaxed and casual.

Café Jaffa
Olei Zion 11, Jaffa (flea market area) * 057- 9439631
Sun – Thurs 9:00 – 24:00, Fri 8:00 – an hour before Shabat

Kosher (dairy). A big, bright space serving good pizzas, pastas, calzones etc. Some fish, but perdominantly vegetarian. It draws a mixed crowd of old and young, trendy and non-trendy, etc. - a pretty random mix resulting in a fun atmosphere. The restaurant is well located for all the excitement of the trendier part of the flea market and often plays host to live music of various kinds. Not alternative, but often odd.

Pasta Basta
Allenby 60 (other side of building, near entrance to Carmel Market) * Sun – Thur 10:00 – 00:00, Fri 12:00 – 16:00

Kosher (dairy). Good sized portions of decent, super cheap pasta (20-30 depending on sauce), cheap desserts and a fun, young vibe. The most awesome thing about this place, though, is the fact that you can get your first bottle of house wine for 35NIS and each "refill" (additional bottle of wine) for 25NIS.

La Lasagna
Dizengoff 177 * 03-5230037 * Sun – Thur 10:00 – last customer,
Fri 10:00 – Shabat, Sat from end of Shabat – last customer

Kosher (dairy). This place has simple décor and no real vibe but offers huge portions of delicious, cheap pizzas, pastas, calzones and lasagnas. You can even opt for healthier whole wheat pasta.

***

There are more pizza places in the **Buy food. Eat Food** section.

Spanish / tapas

None of these are Kosher.

Metushelach
http://metushelach.co.il/ (Hebrew only)
Uriel Acosta 16 * Phone: 03 – 6811018
Sun – Thurs 10:30 – 1:00, Fri 9:00 – Shabat, Sat 19:00 – 1:00
Business deal Sun-Thurs 12:00 – 19:00

This trendy wine bar / tapas restaurant is surprisingly upmarket for Florentin, though still relaxed and casual with a great party atmosphere set to a soundtrack of Balkan, gypsy and 90s rock music. It offers a superb choice of boutique wines (local and international), as well as excellent tapas dishes from various traditions (Spanish, Greek, Italian and more). They also do breakfast during the day (until 17:00) when things are somewhat calmer. If you like your meat and fish, try the Russian breakfast. It comes with vodka. Finding this place is half the fun, as it's pretty small and tucked away in a little cobbled street that comes off another small street. Personally, I think that just adds to its mystique.

Vicky Cristina
http://vicky-cristina.co.il (Hebrew only)
http://bit.ly/r158SR (with English menu)
Hatachana shopping area * 03-7367272 * 12:00 – last customer
daily

A romantic and somewhat upmarket outdoors place designed to
be "authentic" and spread across two separate areas – a tapas
restaurant and a wine bar. They serve various Catalonian tapas
and sea food, with a good choice of salad and other veggie
dishes too. In keeping with the Spanish vibe, the music is also
Spanish.

Asian

Don't expect too much in the way of authenticity. Chefs in Israel's
Asian restaurant go for Asian fusion more often than not. That
said, there's some nice food to be had.

Bait Thailandi
http://www.2eat.co.il/eng/thai
Bograshov 8 (corner of Ben Yehuda) * 03-5178568
Sun – Sat 12:00 – 23:00

Thai (Not Kosher). This tropical-themed restaurant is Tel Aviv's
best and most authentic Thai place. It's always busy. You can
choose how hot you want your food (from mild to Thai grade
super-hot) and also substitute tofu in many of the dishes to make
them vegetarian / vegan. They also do a wicked house shake
which you can have with rum for a very reasonable price.

Moon
Bograshov 58 * 03-6291155 * 12:00 – 3:00 daily
Lunch deals 12:00 – 18:00 daily

Japanese (not Kosher). The first sushi place in Israel to have that cool conveyer belt for your sushi to travel round on. It's modern and stylish and can get very busy, so you may want to make a reservation. It has a very interesting menu with some locally unique fusion sushi alongside more traditional dishes. The menu features lots of vegetarian options and even some stuff for people who don't like sushi.

24 Rupee
http://www.24rupee.com (Hebrew only)
Shocken 16, second floor * 03-6818066 * Sun – Thurs, Sat 12:00 – 00:00, Fri 12:00 – 17:00

Vegetarian Indian. You'll think you got the wrong building when you get to this place, but once you climb up the stairs you'll discover a hidden gem of everything that's good about backpacking in India. It's totally worth the trip to the south of the city for the experience. They make great, cheap thalis with a constantly changing menu plus amazing chai and desserts. The place is decked out in brightly coloured cushions, rugs and throws and has a lovely vibe – just like an Indian guesthouse. Take your shoes off at the entrance and if there are more than 5 of you, it won't hurt to call ahead to book a table.

Zepra
http://zepra.co.il (Hebrew only but maybe adding English soon)
Yigal Alon 96 * 03-6240044 * 12:00 – 00:00 daily

Various Asian fusion (not Kosher). A stylish, bright, loud and colourful place serving all kinds of Asian dishes from noodles to Bangladeshi style curries - mostly various mundane and exotic meats (including ostrich), fish and seafood but also a few good veggie things. The food is great, the juices and desserts are particularly brilliant and the service is super friendly. It's not the cheapest but not really overpriced either and is well worth the money, plus they have a pretty decent business lunch deal. It's a bit out of the way, located in a fairly commercial part of town not far from the Azrieli centre, but is popular with businessmen during lunch and large groups for dinner.

The Bun
Hilel Hazaken 18 * 03-6044725 * Sun – Thur 12:00 – 23:30, Fri 12:00 – 17:00

Vietnamese / Pan Asian (Not Kosher) This cute restaurant at the top of the Carmel market has bar style seating and serves fun Asian food with a Vietnamese slant. If you eat fish, try their excellent salads (they have some fish sauce in them), otherwise, ask for the range of 100% veggie/vegan dishes, including the famous buns.

Dim Sum 33
Mizrahi 33 (corner of Wolfson 5) * 054-201-9792 * Sun – Fri 12:30- 22:00

As the name would suggest, this small and simple place serves great steamed dim sum, either vegetarian / vegan or with beef and chicken. You can sit and eat in (functional but not that exciting) or get a takeaway.

Sing Long
Salame 134 * 03-5375184 * 12:00 – 24:00 daily

Chinese (Not Kosher) The crumbling Shapira neighbourhood might seem like an odd place for a Chinese restaurant, but maybe not when you consider that much of Tel Aviv's foreign worker population lives in the area. The setting is glorified worker restaurant style, the service is friendly and the food is tasty and authentic. There are plenty of veggie and vegan choices, especially when you consider the fact that you can have most dishes made with tofu instead of meat.

Long Seng
Allenby 13 * 03-5163796 * 12:00-15:30 and 18:00-23:00

Chinese (Not Kosher). Not to be confused with the above, this long-established place has a somewhat nicer setting and highly authentic food with two menus – a simplified one in Hebrew aimed at Western tastes and a more interesting one in Chinese and English. There are good veggie and vegan options, though people mostly come here for pork and seafood. Their chow mein dishes come served on top of crispy dough, rather than noodles, and are awesome.

Hanoi
Lilienblum 18 * 03-5337962 * Mon – Sat 18:00 – 24:00

Not Kosher. Yummy Vietnamese and Malaysian dishes (from dim sum to curry), cool design inspired by Asian food markets and reasonable prices make this place insanely popular, so you may want to book a place in advance, even though the place itself is very casual and fun. Good options for meat & fish eaters as well as vegans.

See the **Buy Food. Eat food** section for Asian fast food and takeaway places.

Vegetarian / Vegan

Buddha Burgers
http://www.buddhaburgers.co.il
Yehuda Halevi 21 * 03-5101222/333
Sun-Thurs 11:00 – 24:00, Fri 11:00 – Shabat, Sat 19:00 – 24:00
Ibn Gabirol 86 * 03-5223040
Sun-Thurs 11:00 – 23:00, Fri 11:00 – 17:00

Cheap vegan comfort food and great shakes. Meal options include burritos, burgers, salads, sushi, sandwiches and soups and there are also some raw food options. The Ibn Gavirol branch is more of a takeaway, fast-food place with minimal seating, while the main branch is more like a simple, self-service restaurant and offers cheap beer, wine and cocktails too (though it's not really a getting wrecked sort of place). On Fridays there's a big all you can eat buffet for brunch.

Café Birenbaum
Nahalat Binyamin 31 * 03-5600066 * Sun – Fri 7:00 – 16:00

Kosher dairy / (mostly) vegetarian. This place quite deservedly won the Time Out 2009 award for best value healthy / vegetarian meal in Tel Aviv. Their vegetarian lunch buffet is simply divine with enough delicious, healthy hot food and salads to keep you going for days. All this costs 45NIS per person and you can add (big) desserts for 20NIS more. Drinks are not included, though free pitchers of water are readily given. The place has been around since 1962 and is owned and run by two lovely lovely sisters. The walls are covered with original artwork, including work by Kadishman dedicated to the ladies themselves. Although just off the famed pedestrianised area, it's still a fun and friendly place to sit.

Aba Gil
Yehuda Halevi 55 * 03-5663320 * Sun – Thurs 9:30 – around 5:00, Fri 9:30 – 15:30

This place may look simple, but it serves really great food and is relaxed and hassle-free. The business deal is really good value – a giant plate for 42NIS with delicious hummus, salads (both veg and healthy grains like quinoa, etc.) and pita bread, accompanied by your choice of either quiche or falafel (all organic). It even includes a free soft drink. You can upgrade to a freshly squeezed juice for an extra 8NIS. I dare you to finish all this and stay hungry, but they also make surprisingly good vegan desserts, including the most amazing date and coconut cookies and vegan ice cream. You can also buy fair trade products here, including olive oil, dried fruit and spices.

Mezze
Achad Haam 51A * 03-6299753 * Sun – Thurs 8:00 – 00:00, Fri 8:00 – 17:30

(Mostly) Vegetarian. As the name suggests, this popular bistro/café style restaurant specialises in mezze – the Middle Eastern form of tapas. There's a huge choice of healthy veggie food, great desserts and lots of vegan and gluten free options (90% of the menu is gluten free). Their tahine sauce is legendary and made in many different variations.

Ta'am Hachayim (taste of life)
http://www.tasteoflifeisrael.com
Ben Yehuda 43 * 03-5168906
Sun – Thurs 9:00 – 21:00, Fri 9:00 – 15:00 (14:00 in winter)

A very pleasant place run by the African Hebrew community offering cheap vegan food. They serve many fake meat things, interesting quiches and a variety of raw foods and soya ice cream. Many of the ingredients are organically grown by the Hebrews themselves.

Zakaim
Allenby 98, corner of Simtat Beit Hashoeva 20 * 03-6135060 * zakaimorginal@gmail.com * 12:00 – 00:00 daily

The jury's still out about this place, the product of the local vegan hipster trend, but it's definitely the prettiest and most upmarket place in town to have a 100% vegan dinner. The food is expensive, though tasty (the chips and the desserts are particularly popular) but the menu's somewhat pretentious wording hides a fairly basic range of dishes. On the other hand, the atmosphere and décor are lovely, in a trendy retro-chic sort of way.

***

See the **Buy Food. Eat food** section for more vegetarian and vegan options (fast food, takeaway, street food, etc.). Also check out the **Bar Kayma** in the Bars with good food section.

Various Jewish home-cooked meals

Keton
Dizengoff 145 * 03-5233679 * 12:00 – 22:00 daily

Classic home-cooked East European Jewish cuisine served at this historic restaurant that has fed some of Israel's greatest thinkers throughout its history. Lots of meat, as expected, but also some simple, consciously veggie options.

Bat Artzi
Hashomer 7 * 03 – 5177808
Sun – Thurs 10:00 – 00:00 Fri 9:00 – hour before Shabat (or till the food runs out)

The food in this self-service, co-op run restaurant is just the way your mom would make it, if she were from any of the represented Jewish traditions. There's Iraqi food, Moroccan, Hungarian, Ethiopian, Lebanese, Kurdish, Turkish, Persian and more. Lots of meat and fish stuff (Jewish cuisine is very heavy in both) but the occasional veggie main as well as some veggie and vegan side dishes to make into a meal. If all else fails, there's hummus. The menu changes daily and prices are low.

Mexican

Mexicana
http://www.mexicana.co.il
Bograshov 7 (corner of Ben Yehuda) * 03-5279911 * 12:00 – 00:00 daily

This place has been around since 2006 (a long time for Tel Aviv) and offers decent Tex Mex style food with classic and simple Mexican eatery décor and vibe. Not cheap, but portions are big.

Donkey
Hahashmonaim 91 (corner of Carlibach) * 03-5465295 * 11:30 – 23:30 daily

This popular place is set up like a trendy taqueria / fast food joint and offers healthy(ish) versions of the usual dishes – tacos, burritos, etc. in keeping with the global "fresh mex" trend.

Mezcal
Vital 2* 03-518-7925 * Sun – Thurs 18:00 – 2:30, Fri-Sat 12:00-2:30

This fun tequila bar in the middle of the Florentin bar stretch is known for its large selection of speciality tequilas, good margharitas (including frozen ones) and food which is less Tex Mex and more authentic Mexican (within reason, this is still Israel).

Taqueria
Levontin 28 * 03-6005280 * Sun – Sat 12:00 – 1:00

Do not be fooled by the name, this is a trendy, hip place frequented by aficionados. That said, prices are not insane. Opinions differ as to how authentic the food is, though most agree it's tasty. It gets very busy with cool people, especially on weekends.

African

Tenat
Chlenov 27 * 054-7499538 * Sun – Thur 10:00 – 00:00, Fri 10:00-16:00, Sat 19:00 – 00:00

A bright and modern little café-style place just off the east end of Florentin, serving very tasty vegetarian / vegan Ethiopian food at reasonable prices. It draws a mixed crowd of predominantly young, creative locals. You are encouraged to eat with your hands and share, though you can always ask for a fork. Don't miss out on the great dessert.

Savlanut Restaurant

Rosh Pina 2 (Corner of Hagdud Haivry) * Daily 10:00-22:00 (approx)

This great Sudanese place is run by refugees and is friendly, cheap and yummy. There are a few more like it around the area, which has become a bit of an "Africa town" in recent years. 20NIS will buy you a full veggie/vegan meal of stuff like lentils, spiced beans, veg and bread (with or without cheese) and you can have meat, fish or chicken too (depending on what's available). I've been told not to try the meat here, though as a vegetarian I can't confirm or deny. There's a little garden to sit in, or you can sit in the very colourful restaurant itself.

There is also a decent Eritrean restaurant on the corner opposite the **Sing Long** place on Salame St. (see Asian food above). It seems to be open every day.

Blink and you'll miss it

Things in Tel Aviv move fast. Bars and cafés, especially underground ones, burst into the scene and often disappear soon afterwards. This has a lot to do with Tel Aviv's constantly shifting sense of what's cool and hip, but may also have something to do with the law around these parts. Places are allowed to run for a year without applying for a business license, meaning many of the weirder venues don't have to pay attention to legal obligations such as fire exists, noise reduction measures, etc.. When the year's up many places are forced to close for failing to meet the licensing conditions.

Bars and dance bars

Apart from some very obvious dance bars, most Tel Aviv bars will serve more than one function (food, mingling, dancing, etc.) I've divided up the bars according to what I see as the main function of each.

Israeli Drinking habits

Israelis predominantly drink beer, wine (with their meal) and spirits in shots. Sparkling wine is also fairly popular and is often cheap. You can usually order a single shot of spirits as a "chaser" once you've ordered a beer and then it's cheaper than ordering a "shot". Many places have special offers on the above combination, which is highly popular here. Mixed drinks (i.e. vodka with a soft drink on top) are readily available but if you want one, get ready to get royally shafted in the vast majority of places. Most places treat even the simplest of mixed drinks like some kind of exotic cocktail and charge you accordingly. It's sometimes actually cheaper to get a chaser and a soft drink separately and mix them up yourself. The most popular combinations are vodka & redbull (or a local equivalent energy drink) and arak (Lebanese ouzo) & grapefruit. These sometimes escape the blatant overpricing and are so popular you can even buy them from some juice stalls and kiosks. Arak and grapefruit is likely to be the cheapest mixed drink you can have anywhere – handy if you like aniseed.

Some places still don't measure shots for mixed drinks, but the more commercial (and / or pretentious and overhyped) places increasingly do and the habit is spreading. As for beer, the most common local varieties are Maccabi and Goldstar. Israelis will always tell you that Goldstar is better, but some of my lager-loving English friends actually preferred Maccabi when introduced to both. You can also get a decent variety of imported bottled and draught beers in most places and an increasing number of Israeli boutique beers. The range varies from place to place, with many places even offering stouts like Guinness and Murphy's. I can't guarantee you'll always get someone who can pull a decent pint, though.

Israel uses the metric system, so beers are sold in thirds (shlish) and halves (hetsi) of a litre. A half is sort of like a pint while a third is as close as you'll get to a half pint. **Buying a third is often a giant rip off.** Many bars will sell you a half for only a few shekels more, but don't expect bar staff to volunteer that info. Always ask for the price of a half litre, even if you only want a third.

Dance Bars

Like nightclubs but smaller and usually free to get into (or very cheap).

Anna Loulou Bar
Hapninim 1, Jaffa (a turning off Yefet 17) *
anna.loulou.bar@gmail.com * Mon – Sat 21:00 – late

This lovely little dance bar is easily the coolest place in Jaffa's old city. It's set in a big old arch on the eastern edge of it. The bar has two rooms – one with a big bar and a small performance space hosting frequent intimate gigs and another in the back with comfy sofas. The music ranges from electronic to world to alternative rock with occasional other stuff thrown in. The crowd is a mix of young hipsters from Tel Aviv and cool Jewish and Arab Jaffa residents. Note that this place is very loud and quite relaxed about smoking so gets very very smoky.

Shesek
Lilienblum 17 * 03-5169520 * 21:00 – late daily

This lounge bar has a small dance floor, great retro 70s décor and good DJs playing every night. All nights are free. The eclectic music policy ranges from house to disco, soul, funk and even indie rock. It's a good place to check out if you want to party but don't know where. All nights are free. Note that this place is closing down soon. Check it out while you can.

Michatronix
Ben Yehuda 28 * 054-6402840 * Sun – Thurs, Sat 21:00 – late, Fri 22:00 – late

This place used to be a TV repair shop or something but is now a hip bar with a predominantly young crowd and various party nights, all with a great vibe and usually free. Sometimes there are even live acts playing and then it's even cooler. Music varies but there's plenty of electronica, as well as weird 80s nostalgia, Balkan / gypsy and other random things.

Radio EPGB
Shadal 7 (in the basement) * 03-5603636 * 9:00PM – 7:00AM daily

This popular dance bar used to be cooler and on some early and midweek nights you can still hang out with some cool locals here. On Thursdays and Fridays, though, it's gone a tad more mainstream. The musical line up is always good though and varies from alternative rock to electronica and even dancehall and dubstep. There are often live gigs here too. All free. Relaxed smoking policy.

Frenkel 13

https://www.facebook.com/Frenkel13
Frenkel 13 * 21:30 – 5:00 nightly

A great line up of DJs playing every night (soul, funk, jazz, electronica, rock and more). Regular gigs and even a ping pong table and a library (!) make this place a fun addition to the Florentin nightlife scene. All events are free.

Deli

https://www.facebook.com/deli.telaviv
Allenby 47 * 0545204944 * nightly

A hidden bar at the back of a good sandwich place / diner. Good DJs play almost every night and entry is generally free. The music is generally house / tech house / electro / eclectic with occasional dark 80s. Beware of heavy cigarette smoke, if that bothers you.

Soda Bar

Nahalat Binyamin 43 * 20:00 – 4:00 daily

This bar used to be the big thing in town and while those days are gone, it's still a decent smoky hipster place to check out when you're in the area. DJs play every night, from electronica to disco and loads more. Sometimes there are special events / gigs here.

Bars with live music (almost) every night

Rothschild 12
Rothschild 12 * 03-5106430 * 19:00 – late every day but Friday.

A very stylishly modern gourmet bar set in an old semi-derelict building. To be honest, it's expensive and somewhat pretentious - full of yuppies who like to pretend they're underground without going anywhere *too* gritty. It does, however, have a fun, lively atmosphere and good food and is a brilliant place to catch intimate gigs. It hosts nightly (short) shows by local alternative live acts and they are all free apart from the occasional big events which are still very cheap. There is now also a café in the building that's open during the day with good breakfast and lunch deals.

Tsuzamen
http://tsuzamenbar.com (Hebrew only)
Lilienblum 25 * tsuzamen@gmail.com * 20:00 – late nightly.
Some special events on Friday afternoons

A fun and tiny place hosting a variety of intimate gigs by local bands. Some alternative, some more middle of the road – rock, pop, funk, whatever. Most gigs are free and the rest are cheap.

Tachles Bar
https://www.facebook.com/tachles.bar
Bar Yohai 7 * 0549496336 * tachleslive@gmail.com

This little neighbourhood bar just south of Florentin is great for catching small scale local rock and blues acts several times a week. Check their Facebook page to see what's on (usually Hebrew only). All events are free.

Beit Haamudim
Rambam 14 * 0522222657 * Sun – Thurs 9:00 – 23:00, Fri 9:00 – 17:30, Sat 18:00 – 23:00

Offering live jazz shows almost every night (around 21:30ish), this place is a retro chic bar / café / restaurant with cheap Mediterranean food, cute décor and a chilled vibe. It's also the perfect place to spend a pleasant afternoon, as it's open fronted and overlooks the Nahalat Binyamin pedestrianised area.

Bar Giyora
http://www.bargiyora.co.il (Hebrew only)
Bar Giyora 4 * 03-6204880 * Sun – Thur 9:00 – 1:00, Sat 1:00 – 1:00

This centrally located place (next door to Dizengoff Center) is not at all "alternative", but great for catching more mainstream rock, pop and blues gigs by both new and established local acts. Some gigs are free, some not. Monday nights are open mic nights.

Mingling, hanging out

Places where you can have a quiet drink, grab some simple food, do some people watching and maybe make some new friends (or "special" friends).

Bata vegariga
Lavontin 2 (on the corner with Allenby) * 03-6850493
24 hours a day from Sun 6:00 – Fri 17:00, Sat 10:00 – 00:00

A cosy and beautiful lesbian-owned place (owned by the same people who own **Joz veLoz**, see Restaurant section) with limited inside seating and lots of outside seating for the smokers. Acts as a café during the morning and by afternoon it turns into a bar / café and starts serving booze. It's a lovely place to sit with current alternative music, friendly staff and some interesting food choices. They serve Taybe beer from the world's first (and only) Palestinian microbrewery and a lovely house cocktail. The crowd is mixed gay / straight in their 20s-40s+ and fashionably alternative. The vibe is chilled but lively.

Minzar
Allenby 60 (down the side of the building) * 03-5173015 * Around the clock

This ultimate neighbourhood bar has seemingly been around since the dawn of time and is same as it ever was - friendly, smokey, relaxed and somewhat grubby. The same rock soundtrack is usually still in the background and even the simple, comfort food menu hasn't changed in years. The crowd too is still the same mix of pretty young things on their way out on the town and older locals in casuals grabbing a few before bed. You could turn up looking any way you want and no one will give a shit. It gets very busy and loud on Thursday nights and weekends, at other times it's pretty laid back.

Hoodna
Abarbanel 13 * 03-5184558 * Sun- Thurs 6:00PM – late, Fri & Sat 1:00PM – late

A bar with a cult following of people in their late 20s – 40s, this underground-looking place is split across two low, semi-derelict buildings separated by an alley that looks like something out of a favela. It draws a good crowd all week and occasionally shows big local or international football games on a big screen in one of the spaces (in the week) or hosts free indie gigs (on weekends). At other times it plays a good range of alternative music, old and new. The place is busy most nights and incredibly so on Thursday and Friday nights. Come early if you want happy hour prices and late if you want good atmosphere and people watching. Note that prices are more expensive than you'd expect from the looks of the place, but it's a fun place to hang out (especially now they seem to have sorted out their rude bar staff issues). The same people who own this place own the **Casbah** café (see below).

Silon
King George 89 * 03-6200053
Sun – Thurs 18:00 – last customer, Fri – Sat 21:00 – last customer

A friendly, intimate place with low lighting, terracotta coloured walls and a good choice of beer (including a decent pint of draught Guinness) and other booze. There's also a basic but pleasant range of bar food, a good mix of music from electro to alternative rock (at perfect conversational volume) and a good, chilled crowd of late 20somethings and up.

CorDuroy United
Allenby 99 * nightly. DJs play from about 22:00 – late

This sweet little place is great for a chilled drink in the week, with a friendly, intimate vibe, a fun crowd of hip locals and DJs playing various hipster-loved music nightly at a reasonable volume. On Thursdays and Fridays things get busier with more of a party vibe.

Shpagat
Nahalat Binyamin 43 * 03-5601758 * 21:00 – last customer daily

Officially a gay bar, but in practice multisexual, this hip and relaxed loft-style bar has various party nights for girls and boys and occasional live music from jazz to indie pop. Otherwise just a great place to have a pleasant drink if you want to be surrounded by cool people and be able to hear what they're saying. They enforce the smoking ban.

Uganda
Simtat Beit Habad (just off the corner of Herzl and Derech Jaffa), at the exact point where it bends * Sun-Wed 17:00 – 00:00, Thurs,Fri from 12:00 - late, Sat from 19:00 - late

The little sister of the famous Jerusalem underground phenomenon is not quite as happening as the original, but it's a pleasant enough place to have a quiet drink and listen to good alternative music. Sometimes you can also catch an intimate underground gig or a cool launch here and there is also a cool record/CD/Magazine store. Most of the seating is outside, though there are a couple of sofas and bar seating inside.

Alla Rampa
Ha'Amal 21 * 03-5461506 * 19:00 – 4:00 daily

A busy and trendy bar set in a light industrial area popular with local artists and creatives. Apart from a sort of timeless playlist (jazz, indie rock, random) it offers good food (if not cheap), a varied crowd, occasional live music and the experience of drinking draught beer out of jam jars. Mostly outdoor seating.

Har Sinai
Har Sinai 2 * 21:00 – 3:00 nightly, Thur 21:00 – 4:00, /Fri 22:00 – 44:00

This little, simply designed bar is actually around the bend from Port Said, next door to a good Bulgarian restaurant. I don't personally find it all that exciting, but it's friendly and popular with a very fun young (hipster) crowd. There are DJs playing alternative / hipster music practically every night and booze prices are decent for Tel Aviv. Occasionally there are some pretty cool events here, including book fairs, vintage sales and designer sales. At other times, it's good for a quiet drink and people watching, if you can find a place to sit. Mostly outdoor seating.

Pasáž
Allenby 94 (downstairs) * nightly, sometimes in the day too

This bar / café combo has taken over the entire lower ground floor of the building and has hipster retro décor and DJs playing upbeat hipster music. It's a beautiful space and prices are average for Tel Aviv. The crowd, on the other hand, is mixed – young, older, hip and square. The place is very busy and buzzy at night right now, especially on weekends when there are often gigs and parties, some free, some not. In the day, it's pretty quiet (when open).

Heder 140 (Room 140)
Ben Yehuda 140 * 057-360-0360 * 19:00 – last customer daily. Occasioally also on Friday afternoons for special events.

A little piece of south Tel Aviv transplanted in the heart of tourist country. This great little underground bar has that artfully cobbled together design, comfy sofas, great music from chilled electronica to hardcore techno and alternative rock (delivered by different DJs nightly) and a whole range of speciality aniseed flavoured booze behind the bar (alongside your usual Tel Aviv bar selection). It even has some outdoor seating. If you're staying with the area, make it your new home, though it's worth the trip from further south as well.

Africa

Harakevet 18 * 054-2028480 * Nightly from 21:00 – late, sometimes in the day for special events. Plans to open daily soon.

Set across two floors and with a big back garden, this hip place has a bit of everything – DJs playing nightly (electronic to alternative rock and beyond), live alternative music, mingling with some very cool, creative locals in their 20s-40s and even food and a pool table.

HaMaoz

King George 32 * 03-6209458 * Sun – Thur 20:00 – late, Fri 14:00 – late, Sat 18:00 – late

A busy bar with a neighbourhood feel, designed like a flat (with a working shower and stuff like that). It's very popular with the cool kids in and around the centre of town (mid 20s and up) and plays mostly funk, groove and rock. It has a reputation for being a bit of a pick up joint and is very busy and buzzy on Friday afternoons.

Hamaon 4

Hamaon 4 * Mon-Thur 18:00 – 1:00, Fri 20:00 – 1:00, Sat 14:00 – 1:00

Not to be confused with the above, this little neighbourhood bar in a side alley in Florentin is the perfect place for a quiet drink. It's not entirely unlike a cool Tel Aviv living room, with tastefully thrown-together décor, including chairs made out of the famous green plastic crates seen all over town. There are reasonably priced (and tasty) bar snacks and a fine list of speciality beers to try. The music is played at a very comfortable volume and ranges from alternative to pop and even rockabilly.

Bars with good food

Norma Jean
http://www.2eat.co.il/eng/normajean
Elifelet 23 * 03-6837383 * Sun – Fri 18:30 – last customer, Sat 13:00 – last customer

Part pub, part bistro, this somewhat out of the way place is decked out with some exposed bricks, old-style Guinness adverts and a mind-boggling display of booze, including some rare gems. Loud atmosphere and booze aside, the main draw of the place is the excellent food – mainly meat but with several interesting vegetarian choices (and some good salads for the vegan). The soundtrack is sort of jazzy-bluesy (Tom Waits, Screamin' Jay Hawkins, that kinda thing) and the crowd is mixed, predominantly from late 20s and up to 40s and 50s. The same people who own this place also run the charming and friendly **Norman** (Hillel Hazaken 8 * 03 – 5171030 * Sun – Thurs 18:00 – last customer, Fri 22:00 – last customer, Sat 17:00 – last customer), a small but perfectly stocked bar just next door to the **Galileo Hotel.**

Zevulon the 10th
Zevulun 10 * random opening hours (nights)

A very cool bar / restaurant set up like a Berlin salon, very arty. Serves expensive but very tasty food, booze and even good herbal tea. The place seems to change on a regular basis. Sometimes it's set up more like a restaurant and sometimes more like a bar with live music from jazz bands to surreal acapella singing. Either way, it's OK to just have a drink. The mezzanine floor is a bit notorious for being somewhat of a make out room.

Shafa Bar
Rabbi Nahman 2, Jaffa * 03-6811205
Mon – Thurs 19:00 – late, Fri 12:00 -19:00

A few doors down from the **Shafa hairdressers'** (see Buy stuff section) is this "alternatively alternative" fair-weather bar with its distinctive giant Chinese lantern. The bar's beauty lies in the fact that it's open fronted and its tables are spread along the street and across two spaces, one on each side. The food is tasty, though not cheap, and the music is a fun eclectic mix of oddities. Sometimes there are fun live gigs and street parties out on the street, often on Fridays and Saturdays.

Lior's Place
Florentin 55 (corner of Hahalutsim) * Sun – Thur 12:30 – 00:00, Fri 12:00 - Shabat

Lior is a bit of a Tel Aviv character and his little open-fronted corner bar- restaurant is suitably chilled but a tiny bit crazy. Come here for good, simple local food (from worker style sandwiches to various Middle Eastern dishes and beyond), a pleasant (but small) selection of booze, Turkish coffee and a lovely neighbourhood vibe.

Port Said
Har Sinai 2 * Nightly and soon in the day (hours still not 100% determined)

This bar-restaurant is co-owned by the people who run the Teder (see below) and is based in its historic location (Teder itself has now moved). As such, it is instantly and effortlessly cool, full of people who want to see and be seen. It offers predminntly outdoor seating, as well as limited bar seating inside. It also features some very tasty food, courtesy of chef Eyal Shani, a very hip crowd and music played predominantly off vinyl records.

Bar Kayma
http://barkayma.co.il (Hebrew only)
Hamashbir 22 * info@barkayma.co.il

Grown out of Israel's version of the Occupy movement, this new co-operative bar/ vegan restaurant draws a nice mixed crowd and has super delicious food at reasonable prices. Service is spaced out but friendly and the music is popular alternative eclectic. It can get a bit loud at night and sometimes there are free live music gig. The place is pleasantly smoking free, but there's a comfortable smoker's patio out back.

Cocktail Bars

Not very popular in Israel, sadly.

Imperial Cocktail Bar
Imperial Hotel, Hayarkon 66 (corner of Trumpeldor) * 18:000 – 3:00 daily

Retro 20s style hotel bar with jazz/ oldies to match and well prepared cocktails. Romantic, dimly lit and very stylish. Relaxed smoking policy.

223
Dizengoff 233 * 18:00 – late daily

A neighbourhood bar suitable for a reasonably upmarket neighbourhood – chic design (they call it 40s style) and a nice urban buzz of media darlings and trendy locals. Good cocktails, separate space for smokers.

Other bars

Café Noga

http://www.cafe-noga.co.il (limited English)

Pinsker 4 * Phone: 03- 6296457 Opening hours: Sun – Sat 12:00 – very late Happy hour: till 21:00

Tel Aviv's friendliest, loudest and craziest pool / snooker / billiards / darts / sports bar that exists so far outside of cool, it's almost cool. It's been there since the 80s and not much has changed, including the menu and the prices. In spite of its name, it's decidedly not a café in any way but very much a bar, serving your usual booze and basic bar comfort food to keep you going while you play. The music is mostly classic rock of various kinds and there's an interesting mixed crowd from Tel Aviv and beyond, both young and old.

Teder

http://www.teder.fm

Location changes yearly.

Tel Aviv's own pop up alternative radio station / bar. It's on for a few months in summer offering everything from dancing to food and mingling. This is where all the city's coolest hipsters go almost every single night. As usual, this season's location is also a large outdoors space with some arches around it. Try the alcoholic slushy. It's great.

Cafés

Tel Aviv has a real café culture. There are cafés you'd meet your friends at, ones you'd take your parents to and even ones you'd have business meetings in or simply sit with your laptop and work. Different crowds congregate in each neighbourhood café and most places have their own unique vibe. You'll notice that there are absolutely no Starbucks in Tel Aviv. That's right - they tried and failed to work the Israeli market and were beaten by the excellent local places. Israelis like good coffee and Starbucks just didn't deliver the goods. There are, however, a few big local chains - Aroma, CaféCafé , Café Hilel, Arcaffé, Café Landwer and Cup'o' Joe to name a few, all pretty unexciting, but still better than the big S would have been. Landwer and Joe are probably the most pleasant and Aroma the least – sterile and faceless like a hospital canteen, although the food and the coffee are actually quite pleasant.

On the menu

Popular drinks you can find in Israeli café include **Turkish / Arabic coffee** (short, black and strong, sometimes mixed with cardamom), **chai** (sometimes served as a fancy chai latte), available all year round, **hot apple cider** (non-alcoholic warm apple juice, or the same but mixed with red wine or brandy), **sachlav or sahlev** (see street food section for info) available in the winter months, various iced teas, cafés and alcoholic slushies in the summer months and lots of fresh or dried herbal infusions including mint, sage, lemon balm and white-leaved savoury (zuta). Many cafés, by the way, carry soya milk, though it often costs a little bit more.

Laptop-friendly cafés

Most cafés in Tel Aviv have wifi nowadays, including all the big chains, but I've marked out places that are particularly laptop-friendly in this section. If you're looking for a place to work or study with your laptop, rather than just read emails, you may also want to check out the **Internet** section in the **Useful Stuff** chapter and the **Tours, Workshops, Lectures** section of the **Do Stuff** chapter for more communal workspace options.

Casbah
Florentin 3 * Sun – Sat 9:00 – last customer
Happy hour 17:00 – 21:00

A funky neighbourhood café-bar with cool décor, including changing artwork by local underground artists. The place looks like it was sort of thrown together in an effortlessly cool sort of way – There's arty lighting, somewhat mismatched furniture and lots of tea lights to set the mood. There's also a great outdoor space with wooden decking and lovely, peaceful seating. The music policy is eclectic and there's a very comfortable vibe with people popping in and out, dogs playing under the tables and all-round general niceness. They serve basic café food plus the usual range of hot drinks and booze. Nothing too fancy, but people come here predominantly for the crowd and the atmosphere. You can try the hibiscus, passion fruit soda or Rosetta (almond cordial) if you're feeling adventurous. The same people who own this place own the **Hoodna** (see Bars).

Hanasich Hakatan (The little prince)
littleprince@gmail.com
Nahalat Binyamin 18 (find the door that goes into the building and it's on the top floor) * 03-6299387 * * Sun – Thurs 10:00 – 2:00, Fri 10:00 – late, Sat 19:00 – 2:00

King George 19 * 03-525-3632 * Sun – Thur 10:00 – 22:00, Fri 10:00 – 18:00

Tel Aviv's most bohemian café / bar now has two branches, both of them very bookish and offering a decent choice of all day breakfasts and other light meals. The Nahalat Binyamin branch is a beautiful and unusual space set up like a retro library with a huge, very very sunny balcony. It's airy and bright with a chilled, intellectual atmosphere - great for working with your laptop or just relaxing. It's been there for a while and is now on the shabbier side of shabby chic, but very comfortable and peaceful nonetheless.

The King George branch is newer and functions more as a used bookstore with a good choice of books in English and other languages. The cute café is at the back and there's a pretty garden to sit in too. It's very popular with the laptop crowd. Both locations host all kinds of events in the evenings, though many are things like Hebrew poetry readings and literary magazine launches.

Alby
Hagdud Haivry 8 * Sun – Thurs 8:00 – 00:00, Fri 8:00 – 18:00, Sat 12:00 – 00:00

Friendly, casual and oozing Middle Eastern bohemian activist chic, this lovely queer-run café draws a great local crowd of activists, anarchists, thinkers and creatives. It's a top place to chill, work or have a great cup of coffee and a cheap light meal.

Café Sheleg
Geula 44 (corner of Allenby) * 03-5101710 * Sun – Thurs 7:00 – 00:00, Fri 7:00 – 18:00

This little café is certainly hip. It's set in a listed building with huge windows overlooking the road and is very tastefully decorated in a vaguely retro fashion. It draws a dedicated creative crowd and has a great, relaxed vibe. Food choices are limited but yummy and it's a good place to grab a light breakfast.

Xoho
http://cafexoho.rest-e.co.il *
https://www.facebook.com/CafeXoho
Mapu 18 (corner of Ben Yehuda) * 072-2495497 * Sun – Wed 8:00 – 21:00, Thurs 8:00 – 00:00, Fri 9:00 – 16:00

A neighbourhood café with an arty, laid back vibe. It seems to draw out the local English speaking crowd and has a definite community spirit with regulars seeing it as their second home. The menu is pescatarian / vegetarian and there are often intimate gigs, open mic nights and various other events here in the evenings.

The Streets
King George 70 * 077-3511513 * Sun – Fri 7:30 – 4:00, Sat 9:00 – 4:00

Bacio
King George 85 * 03-5289753 * Sun 0 Thur 8:00 – 24:00, Fri 8:00 – 14:00, Sat 16:00 – 24:00

These two very central places are right across the street from each other. **The Streets** is a big New York style café set across a couple of floors, while **Bacio** is smaller and more intimate (though surprisingly it often has space when The Street doesn't).

143

Both offer a clean, bright and modern design with a decent menu of food options to keep you going while you work. Both local and foreign freelancers and students seem to love these two cafés and if you like the Lev HaIr neighbourhood vibe then you will probably love them too. Personally, I don't find them particularly exciting, though. You'll get more space and better value in the others I've listed here.

Other Cafés

Sonya Getzel Shapira
http://www.rest.co.il/sites/Default.asp?txtRestID=10065
Simta Almonit 1 (entrance is from King George 18, at least for the time being)* 057 – 9442801
Sun – Sat 8:00 – 24:00 (later on Fri night)

This café boasts one of the best café menus in town. It's a relaxed place with a shady garden and a fun menu including good chai and the cutest kids' menu that adults can have too (fish-shaped chocolate sandwiches, aeroplane-shaped cheese toasts, etc.). There's little indoor seating so this is more of a fair weather spot, even though they do cover bits of the garden in winter. Fridays and Saturday lunchtimes get very busy and often involve waiting to be seated.

Casino San Remo
Nehama 2 * 03-5042003 * 7:30 – late daily

This pretty café / restaurant / bar is a popular hipster outpost on the edge of Jaffa (by the Noga theatre) and hosts lots of great music events (parties & gigs), as well as very popular themed world food parties. It's a fun place to hang out, hear some tunes and chill out.

Kaymak

Levinsky 49 (corner of Nahalat Binyamin) * 03-5185228

Flexible hours, sort of 7:00 (ish) – 00:00AM(ish)

This is one of my favourite cafés in town. It is a small oasis bang in the centre of the busy Levinsky market and about 10-15 minutes walk from the central bus station. It looks like a proper open-fronted Turkish or Moroccan café with ornate lampshades, simple flea market furniture and a big ceiling fan whizzing away. Red fez hats decorate the walls and the little stereo plays a funky mix of random music with a distinct Middle Eastern edge. They serve up a good choice of drinks including pots of strong Turkish coffee and nice herbal infusions. There's also very nice veggie food made with stuff from the market – stews, sandwiches, soups and shakshuka (see Street Food section). It can get very busy on Fridays when everyone rushes to the market to do last minute shopping before Shabat. At other times it's pretty relaxed. Kaymak, in case you're wondering, is a type of sweet cheese / curd Turkish dish that's now sadly gone from the menu. It does has free wifi, but is often too busy to be able to handle people working for hours on their laptops.

Pua

http://www.rol.co.il/sites/eng/puaa

Rabbi Yohanan 8, Jaffa * Sun – Wed 10:00 – 24:00, Thurs – Sat 24 hours.

This beautiful shabby-chic café is in the middle of the Jaffa flea market and doubles as an antique store, so if you wanted to you could buy the chairs you're sitting on, the lights off the ceiling and your plates and glasses. The food is unpretentious and yummy with a home-cooked feel and the crowd is a mix of arty people from the nearby stores, bohemian market goers and tourists off the old Jaffa trail.

HaMeshulash
Dizengoff 168 * 03-5236734 * Sun – Wed 8:00 – 3:00, Thur – Sat 24 hours.
Business deal: Sun – Thurs 12:00 -17:00

Has a decidedly more unbuttoned vibe than most places on Dizengoff and is blatantly unpretentious. It has a young, fun atmosphere, especially on Fridays and Saturdays, when it can get quite busy.

Segafredo
Dizengoff 106 * 03-5238257 * 24 / 7

Segafredo is actually the brand of coffee they sell, but that's what everyone calls this place. They have a particularly good take away menu and offer cheap "mini sandwiches" that are very good value if you want a cheap snack with your coffee. They also serve very lovely cakes and chocolates they make themselves, alongside excellent coffee. The proximity to the Beit Lessin theatre means you'll get to see some locally famous actors chilling out here on their breaks. At other times, it provides a late night or early morning pit stop to the areas cooler (or more peculiar) residents.

Café Salma
https://www.facebook.com/SalmaSCafe
Yehuda Hayamit 34, Jaffa * 03-5259461 \ 052-5679195 * Su – Fri 8:00 – 00:00, Sat 8:00 – 17:00

This very cool little café is where some of Jaffa's coolest and most interesting people hang out and for a good reason. It has a really special neighbourhood feel and hosts some very cool art events and music gigs. If you want to experience a laid back and hip manifestation of Jaffa's cross-cultural vibe, then definitely go hang out there.

Paul's
Yefet 142, Jaffa * 03-5188190, 03-6810143
Sun – Thurs 8:00 – 20:00, Fri 8:00 – 16:00

Jaffa's version of an Italian café is a coffee lover's heaven with a huge variety of freshly ground blends of speciality coffees. They also have a large range of teas and infusions, cakes, breakfast foods, etc. The vibe is the most authentically "Jaffa" you're likely to find – a mix of unpretentious Jews and Arabs casually doing their thing and enjoying their coffee without making a big deal out of it. You can take some ground coffee home with you and you really should. Consult the knowledgeable staff if you're not sure of what to buy.

For more good cafés in Jaffa, check out **Yafa** in the Politics / Places section and the **Margoza Bakery** and **Piece of cake** in the Food section.

Bacio Mersand
Frishman 18 (or Ben Yehuda 70, it's on the corner)
Sun – Thurs 8:00 – 24:00, Fri 7:30 – 18:00, Sat 10:30 – 24:00

You may have heard of Sheinkin Street's historic **Café Tamar.** This is another café that was known as an old people's café (it started off as a young people's café and grew old with its regulars). When the owner passed away, it got bought out but the original retro décor (retro cause it hadn't changed for decades) was left more or less the same, keeping the regulars happy. The place now draws a young, hip crowd, as well as the older generation and has a basic but yummy food selection. If you want a taste of Tel Aviv's more innocent past without being surrounded solely by old people, this is your place. The original retro seating inside is not the most comfortable in town, but certainly authentic.

6 Buy stuff

The magic word is: haggle. Almost every price tag in Tel Aviv is merely a suggestion, with the possible exception of stuff in the big chain stores and supermarkets. Even posh stores will often give you a discount if you ask in the right way (nicely). Israelis will sometimes just ask for a discount straight away, without giving a particular reason for this. As a tourist, you can increase your chances of getting a discount by buying more than one item and asking for the price to be rounded down or simply reduced. As long as you ask nicely, there's no harm in erring on the side of haggling anywhere you go.

Shopping Centres

Dizengoff Center is probably the most famous shopping centre in Tel Aviv and sits on the corner of Dizengoff and King George St.. It's really more useful than exciting, but has some high street brands (Zara, Mango, etc.) as well as their local equivalents which sometimes have nice stuff, plus random little stores that can be fun. The fact that it's set up across two interconnected buildings and several floors makes it a bit more interesting to get lost in. The **Azrieli Center** is a bit out of the real centre of town and is really pretty dull, though it has the Tel Aviv branch of H&M. There's an observation deck on top of one of the buildings, where you can get some far reaching views across the whole of Israel. The weirdest "shopping centre" in Tel Aviv is without a doubt the central bus station building (see **Get Around** section), though you may well totally hate it.

Markets

Dizengoff Center Designer Market
Dizengoff Center, lower ground floor passageway between the buildings (by the food market) * Thurs 16:00- 21:00, Fri 10:00 – 16:00

You can buy clothing and accessories directly from Tel Aviv's hot young fashion designers at this small but packed fashion market. There's some really nice stuff here from the smart but trendy to the outright quirky.

Dizengoff Square Antiques Market
Dizengoff Square * Tues 12:00 – 22:00, Fri 7:00 – 16:00

A small antiques market with stalls selling weird and wonderful antiques, collectibles, jewellery, toys and even some clothes. There's usually lots of interesting Israeli nostalgia stuff. Prices are generally not insane.

Shuk Hapishpeshim (Jaffa Flea Market)
Daily apart from Saturday (half day on Fridays)

A largeish area between Amiad, Oley Tsiyon, Yehuda Margoza and Beit Eshel streets in Jaffa. This is still one of the most interesting places to hang out in Tel Aviv, even though it's slowly renewing and becoming somewhat less "real". There are lots of antiques, vintage clothes, furniture, Moroccan rugs, Bauhaus and other antique lights, etc. plus a proper flea market area with all kinds of weird stuff of dubious origin. Look out for the little indoor alleyways with lots more surprises. You'll need to haggle hard to get any decent deals in the market, which is quite a tourist trap. The area is very much THE cool place to be right now (well, one of them anyway), with cool late night bars, restaurants and cafés all around. Check out **Pua, Café Jaffa** and **Bar Shafa** in the Eat Out, Drink Out section.

Nahalat Binyamin
Nahalat Binyamin pedestrianised area
Tuesdays and Fridays 10:00 – 17:00

Tel Aviv's crafts market takes over the Nahalat Binyamin pedestrianised area twice a week (unless it's raining). Friday is usually the busier day. The market is super touristy and has its fair share of tacky tourist stuff, but there's actually some really good stuff too – original jewellery and other cool handmade things that make good gifts.

Neve Shaanan
Neve Shaanan St. near the central bus station
Daily (busiest day is Saturday)

If you like the vibe you get in semi – rough, multicultural immigrant neighbourhoods then head down to this jumble sale – like market, frequented mostly by African refugees and migrant workers from the Far East and South America. It offers random new, second hand and stolen goods, Thai and Filipino street food and plenty of weird little eateries and exotic supermarkets to explore. Everything is cheap. It's best to go in the day as this place is not very pleasat at night (plus the market shuts in the evening).

Clothes / shoes / accessories

Areas

Dizengoff St.

This was Tel Aviv's original shopping street and it has retained its bourgeois charm to this day, more or less. While flush with designer stores it's nonetheless more accessible than Kikar Hamedina, Tel Aviv's luxury brand area, where the super-rich can go and spend $4000 on a bag. The majority of the stores here are predominantly aimed at trendy yuppies buying beyond their means, rather than millionaires. The main designer store area starts around the intersection with Frishman St. and stretches north practically to the end of Dizengoff. There are lots of shoe stores, trendy young designer and imported fashion stores, plus lots of smart clothes and bridal wear (that's the only time normal Israelis allow themselves to spend lots of money on smart clothes). In between are a few cheaper clothing stores and the occasional vintage place. You could easily spend several hours and a few thousand NIS here if you had the time and inclination.

Gan Hachashmal

Tel Aviv's young (but already big) fashion designer area spreads around Gan Hachashmal (Gan Hasharon) and the surrounding streets. Clothing, shoes, jewllery and accessories are all well-catered for. You can pick up a map of the area and its shops from any of the designer stores in the area. If you're looking for Tel Aviv's most unique designer offerings, this is probably where you'll find them, but they won't be cheap. The place is undergoing change at the moment and rents are going up, meaning designers are really struggling. Go now before it's gone.

Sheinkin

It used to be Tel Aviv's coolest street when I was a teenager and while it's nothing of the sort nowadays, it still makes for some cool shopping. There are a few good vintage stores, a few good designer stores and trendy boutiques and even a few places selling Indian imports. Several of Tel Aviv's trendiest shoe places have branches here, so it's a good street to cover if you want to take a lot in and are short of time. If you're in the Sheinkin area, you should also check out the parallel Merkaz Baalei Hamelacha Street, starting at the King George end (it gets residential and dull after that). King George itself is good for cheap clothes, shoes and swimsuits.

Tchernihovsky

This neat residential street has a surprising amount of funky little boutiques – vintage, designer and streetwear for men and women, as well as some very cool shoes. It's not very big and is conveniently located (between Allenby and Bograshov) so makes for a convenient window-shopping route on the way from A to B.

Allenby

A blast from the past with all kinds of weird, cheap stores from clothes to books, musical instruments and much more. It's grubby, busy and rundown but will show you a different, less touristy side of the city. Check out the over the top evening wear stores with their sequin and crystal finery. There are also a few places selling bling that wouldn't shame a burlesque starlet.

King George

Good for street/clubby clothes, hippie clothes, swimsuits and cheap lingerie. Near the Sheinkin end is the Bezalel Market, which is great for cheap clothes if you need something basic and can't afford to spend loads of money (tracksuits, tops, sweatshirts/jumpers, swimsuits, etc.).

Bograshov

Good for second hand and vintage clothes stores as well as street clothes and young fashion. Also good if you happen to need wallpaper.

HaTachana

http://www.hatachana.co.il * Sun – Thurs, Sat 10:00 - 22:00, Fri 10:00 -17:00 * Between Neve Tzedek and the sea behind Derech Eilat. Entrance to the car park is from HaMered St.

A big, posh and pretentious shopping area on the site of a defunct historic train station. It was basically designed by the city's council to attract rich tourists. It's full of Israeli and foreign designer stores (mostly overpriced but some nice stuff) and various shops aimed at yuppies. It gets horribly busy with awful people on weekends but is good for concentrated designer shopping if you're short of time and have lots of cash to burn. There are also some very nice restaurants onsite. Surprisingly, there's actually a decent organic farmers' market here every Friday morning till 15:00 and also the occasional fashion and art market.

Club / Cyber / Goth / Hippie / Street Clothes

Plazma
http://www.plazmalab.com
King George 8 * 03-6208127 * Sun – Thurs 10:30 – 22:00, Fri 9:00 – 17:00

A neat store stuffed full of funky clubby clothes and accessories by local and international designers – some fluoro (UV reactive) stuff, cool T-shirts and all kinds of unusual things. Not particularly cheap, but not insanely expensive either.

Jiffa
King George 4 * 03-5252005 * Sun – Thur 10:00 – 21:00, Fri 9:30-17:00

Mostly imported clothes, shoes and accessories from cool international urban, skater and street clothes brands. Cool trainers/sneakers, hoodies, dresses and club clothes.

Salon Berlin
Najara 15 * 03-5102126 * Sun – Fri 10:00 – 2:00, Sat 20:00 – 2:00

It's a funky fashion boutique (new and vintage clothes), a bar - café and intimate performance space, and also an 80s nostalgia concept store and an art gallery. It draws a regular crowd of young hipsters of both the queer and straight variety and is definitely a part of a very specific local scene.

King George 14

I have no idea what this place is called but they sell loads of nice, cheap Thai fisherman trousers, sarongs, harem trousers, Indian

154

dresses and other hippie clothes – great stuff for the Israeli summer and you can usually get good deals if you buy a few items. Sometimes they are actually cheaper than the nearby Carmel market and they definitely have a bigger choice of cool stuff. In winter they sell pashminas and jumpers / sweaters too.

Nox Fashion
http://www.myspace.com/nox_fashion
Frishman 42 * 03-5278077

Imported street wear, goth, alternative, club fashion and mild fetish clothing (PVC, corsetry, etc.). They also do a good range of shoes from popular international labels such as Pleaser, New Rock, etc. As far as I know, this is the only place in Tel Aviv that imports the stuff they have in stock.

Nani
http://www.nanilee.com
Mohilever 49 (Nahalat Binyamin market area) * 03-5165564
Ben Shetach 12, Jaffa * 077-7516554
Sun- Thurs 9:00 – 19:00, Fri 9:00 – half hour before Shabat.
Opening hours are flexible.

Pretty and sometimes unusual Indian imports – clothes, shoes, jewellery, mirrored and sequined belly dancing outfits, etc. The Jaffa shop sometimes has Indian music, kitran and other Indian events on in the evenings.

Tomer
http://www.tomerposters.co.il(Hebrew only)
Disengoff Center, building A 2nd floor, by gate 7 and 5 * 03-5280651
Sun – Thurs 10:00 – 20:00, Fri 10:00 – 13:00

This little store has been there since the early 80s. It sells band T-shirts and posters, alternative jewellery, patches, badges, etc. They also print stuff on demand. For me, their main appeal is that they occasionally import full-on alternative clothing from abroad that doesn't sell too well locally. They then sell it off cheap so you can get a bargain.

Colors
http://www.airbrush.co.il
Dizengof Center, building A, 2nd floor, shop #404 * 03 – 6209166
Sun – Thurs 11:00 – 21:00, Fri 10:00 – 16:00

This place customises just about anything with traditional style airbrush paintings. They do your usual range of faeries and pixies, superheroes and cartoons, 80s style psychedelia, Americana, manga, etc., plus custom stuff. They paint on clothes, shoes, guitars, laptops, you name it. Lots of tacky stuff for sure, but all skillfully done. Check out the website for pictures.

Vintage and retro clothes

Tel Aviv is full of them. These are just a few...

Mugraby
Allenby 32 * Sun – Thurs 8:30 – 20:00, Fri 8:30 – 17:00

This place has a lovely vibe, almost magical, in fact. There are old jazz songs playing in the background, neat clothes and antiques everywhere and a hassle-free attitude from the sweet people who run the place. They are very much against overpricing second hand goods, which makes them even cooler, as far as I'm concerned. The place also operates as a little café so you can get a coffee here and sit out back. Not the most exciting place, but a good place to leave your non-shopaholic boyfriend while you browse.

Aderet
Bugrashov 53 * 03-6203854 * Sun – Thurs 11:00 - 20:00, Fri 10:00 – 16:00

Local secondhand and some imported vintage for men, women and children. A funky store with only a few rails of stuff but with some good finds.

Eshet Chail
Tchernichovsky 3 * 03 – 6201256
Sun – Thurs 12:00 – 20:00, Fri 10:00 – 17:00

Lots of interesting vintage stuff. Not particularly cheap but a good place to browse and maybe find something special.

Rak Shniya
Levontin 1 * Haavoda 1 * Sheinkin 36 * 03 – 5661346 *
Sun – Thur 10:00 – 20:00, Fri 10:00 – 16:00

Cool, reasonably priced (though not "cheap") vintage, including a whole floor of super-cheap finds at the Levontin branch. Lots of colourful finds, some are redesigns.

Bella Vintage
King George 32 * 077-4002739 * Sun – Thurs 11:00 – 20:00, Fri 11:00 – 17:00

This shop is owned by a friendly collector who charges fair prices based on each item's actual value. Lots of interesting pieces at very reasonable prices including some rare, original Israeli vintage.

Kassima
Nahalat Binyamin 23 (in the courtyard) * 077-5250387 * 10:00 – 24:00

A cute little vintage store that's next door to a cute little café. There are only a few racks, but everything is handpicked and reasonably priced. Check out the bargain rack at the front for some real bargains.

Roni Kantor
Rothschild 64 * 074-7033488 * Sun – Thurs 10:00 – 20:00, Fri 10:00 – 16:30

Not strictly vintage, but one-off redesigns made out of original vintage dresses plus new vintage-inspired designs. Also a very nice line of vintage-inspired shoes (that also happen to be vegan, in case you care). None of it is cheap, as this is technically a designer store, but everything is certainly unique and pretty.

Zaza Yael Kedem
Sheinkin 20 (down the side) * 03-6295857 * Sun – Thurs 10:00 – 20:00, Fri 10:00 – 17:00

Carefully selected clothes and accessories from all over the world with a distinct vintage, slightly hipstery edge. I'm not sure if they're vintage, redesigns, originals or all of the above, but either way, they're very cool and often one-offs.

Ortal Fashion
Hagdud Haivri 4 * Sun – Thur 12:00 – 20:00, Fri 11:00 – 16:00

A small store packed with loads of bold vintage / retro clothes at very cheap prices. The shop is owned and run by a well known and somewhat controversial feminist activist who also offers feminist styling advice for people of all genders and orientations.

Bigudiyot
King George 35 * 03-6206851 * Sun – Thurs 11:00 – 20:00
Brodezki 19, Ramat Aviv * 03-6410165 * Sun – Thurs 8:00 – 12:00
Arlozerov 100 * 03-5230448 * Mon, Tues, Thurs, Fri 9:00 – 13:00, Wed 13:00 – 17:00
David Hamelech Blvd. 38 * 03-6923870 * Sun – Thurs 10:00 – 14:00

Bigudyot is the collective name for these charity /thrift stores, run by Wizo - a women's charity. An individual one is called a Bigudit. Real charity stores are not that common in Israel but these follow the same model you may know from where you're from – lots of clean clothes and shoes arranged mostly by colour and at low low prices. The clothes are donated by people, so are generally second hand, not proper vintage, but every once in a while you find something really good. Supposedly the Ramat Aviv branch is good for designer clothes.

Finders Keepers

Tel Aviv is an amazing place for finding random things in the street. People tend to leave perfectly wearable second hand clothes on benches, or in neat piles by a bin. Sometimes, they're even freshly washed. You can also often find books, furniture and other interesting things lying in the street. I know people who've furnished whole flats with stuff they've found outside and I have a few vintage street finds in my wardrobe myself. Happy hunting!

Designer Clothing and accessories

Frau Blau
http://www.fraublau.com/index.php
HaHashmal 8 * 03- 5601735

Cutting edge clothing (for Israel), sometimes inspired by punk, cyber, fetish or retro fashion. They are particularly known for their innovative use of printed effects to create unusual illusion items.

Tomer Ben Cnaan
http://www.facebook.com/tomerbencnaan
Allenby 92 * 0522-577421 * Mon – Thur 12:00- 19:00, Fri 10:00 – 16:00 *

A design studio selling original clothes for women (and some cool T shirts for men) at very sane prices – practically all of them are made on site. The clothes are pure Tel Aviv – flattering, slick and versatile dresses and separates that can be worn either casual or smart, made of high quality materials with a quirky, modern edge. There are also original urban accessories for sale.

Anjaly
http://www.anjaly.com
Mikve Israel 10 * 03- 6868733

Pretty designer yoga clothes (and yoga inspired clothes) for men and women made from organic cotton. Made to breathe and last.

Doron Ashkenazi
Dizengoff 187 * 03-5272679

"Urban tailoring" for men, i.e. great smart casual and smart clothes for fashion-conscious metrosexuals (and women who like to wear men's clothes).

Naama Betsalel
http://www.naamabezalel.com (Hebrew only)
Dizengoff 212 * 03-5232964
Sale store - Dizengoff 234 * 03-5442689

Young but respectable retro-inspired clothing and accessories. Lots of well-made, flattering designs for women but a bit overpriced for what it is.

Hamartef
King George 2 * 03-5283659 * Sun – Thurs 10:30 – 19:00, Fri 10:30 – 15:00

This unassuming place almost at the corner with Sheinkin St. sells discounted past season designer shoes and clothes. A good place to pick up a cheap(ish) pair of Prada heels.

Jus / Plastic Doll

Yohanan Hasandlar 14 (corner of Sheinkin 30) * 0545454202 *
Sun – Thur 11:00 – 19:00, Fri 10:00-15:00

Punk rock / trashy style clothes for women (and a bit for men).
Lots of skulls, pop icons, stars and unicorns. Hot.

Ugly Duckling

http://www.gal-angel.com
Home Studio at Pinsker 13 by appointment only * hello@gal-angel.com * 052-256-8801

Lovely, retro-chic designer swimwear and longewear, with very
flattering cuts. Predominantly for women. Prices are definitely
designer prices.

Guy Gil

http://www.facebook.com/guygilcohen
Sheinkin 34 * guygilcohen@gmail.com

Big, bold, crazy and beautiful plastic jewellery by a talented local
designer. All one of a kind pieces, lovingly handmade. Great for
hipsters, retro/vintage lovers and anyone who likes to make a big
statement with their accessories.

Shoes

In general, you should try Sheinkin St. and Dizengoff St. from the corner with Frishman northwards for a shoe overload. Get your wallets ready!

Shufra
http://www.shoofra.co.il
Dizengoff 108 * 03-5247274
Sun – Thurs 10:00 – 21:00, Fri 10:00 – 16:30

Funky, trendy and designer shoes by local designers and international labels like Fly London, Irregular Choice, etc.. There is another branch on Sheinkin St.

Una Una (achat achat)
http://una-una.com
Rabbi Yohanan 8, Jaffa * 03-5184782

Amazing, mindblowingly cool handmade shoes and not insanely expensive. This is their workshop where they make their shoes and sell them directly to the public. You can also find their shoes in designer stores around town, including Dizengoff St. where they also seem to have their own store now at no. 226.

Katalina Shoes
King George 43 * 03-6291843 * Sun – Thur 10:00-19:30, Fri 10:00-Shabat

Great for reasonably cheap shoes from various local brands of flip flops, sandals, slippers, pumps etc. to Doc Marten-style boots they make themselves (which are vegan and can be made to order in a choice of materials).

Hair and body

Kundalarasta
King George 4 and 44 * 03-6207045, 03-6207044 * Sun – Thurs 10:30 – 21:00, Fri 10:00 – Shabbat.

Two branches of the same company that do hair extensions, braids, plaits and dreadlocks (permanent, temporary and repairs). They also do more standard haircuts, though that's not really what they're known for. Walk-ins are often possible.

Shafa
Nahman 2, Jaffa * 03-5181573
Sun – Wed 10:00 – 19:00, Thurs 10:00 – 23:00, Fri 10:00 – 17:00

These self-taught hairdressers do not too expensive haircuts for men and women in Jaffa's flea market area. Walk-ins are occasionally possible. People come here as much for the vibe as for the style. This is the closest thing you'll get to having your hair cut by a trusted friend. They specialise in freestyle, curly hair cuts and short quirky styles for women rather than slick classic cuts but the experience is fun and you'll get no hard sell on products (a rarity in Tel Aviv). Here's a link to a (Hebrew) blog post showing a pretty haircut they gave someone: http://www.5shekel.com/2011/01/new-haircut.html They also do manicures and pedicures and have a treatment room upstairs with various alternative treatments. There is a **Shafa Bar** too (see bar section).

Vision tattoos
http://www.visiontattoos.co.il
Merkaz Ba'alei melaha 5 (down the side of the building) * 03 –
6201626 * Sun – Thurs 11:00 – 20:00, Fri 11:00 – 16:00

A tattoo place that produces some very fine work. It comes highly
recommended by people I know who got inked there and are
very happy with both the work and the overall experience and
vibe. You can also buy some original artwork by the artists.

Psycho tattoos & piercings
http://www.psychotattoo.com * info@psychotattoo.com
Dizengoff Center, gate 2, 2nd floor (in front of the lifts) * 03 -
6201088

True story: A friend of mine in Tel Aviv wanted a big tattoo done
on her back. She was willing to pay anything and go anywhere to
have it, so she scanned the web for the best international artists.
She found some artwork that blew her away and clicked on the
artist's details, expecting it to be in Japan or somewhere exotic
like that. It turned out to be Avi Vanunu, the guy who founded
this place. The tattoo, by the way, looks incredible. To conclude:
this studio has been around for over 15 years and these guys are
very highly regarded locally and internationally.

Yullia Spa Express
http://yullia.com (Hebrew only)
Dizengoff 101 (corner of Frishman) * 1-700-707-606 * Sun –
Thurs 8:00 – 23:00, Fri 8:00 – afternoon
Herzl 17 (corner of Yehuda Halevy) * Sun – Thurs 8:00 – 20:00,
Fri 8:00 afternoon
Yirmiyahu 43 * Sun – Thurs 8:00 – 20:00, Fri 8:00 afternoon

A chain of fun New York style express spas that are modern,
clean and classy. They offer manicures, pedicures, waxing and

treatments for men and women and are fast and efficient, though a bit more expensive than the smaller places in town. Walk ins generally possible.

Regina Tal
Stern 11 * 054-2340146

A tiny place in Florentin run by two sisters. They offer good, cheap waxing, eyebrow shaping, manicures, pedicures, etc. for women. Call in the daytime for an appointment.

Community Acupnucture
http://www.dikur-yoga.com (Hebrew only apart from contact page)* Contact Maya on 054-4538804 or via website

This lady offers discounted acupuncture treatments where you get a private consultation followed by an acupuncture session in a room with other people. This keeps the prices low and the atmosphere is very friendly. She's good, too.

If you don't like this method of working, you can also opt for more expensive private treatments incorporating acupuncture, yoga, massage and Qigong.

This isn't really a shopping thing, but this version of the guide doesn't have a dedicated complementary medicine section.

Books

Israelis love to read, but the majority of the cool, independent book shops (those that are left) mostly carry Hebrew books. Here are some options for getting books in English and other languages. If you speak English, Russian, French or German you won't have a problem finding something to read in town.

Steimatzky
http://www.steimatzky.co.il (Hebrew only)
Allenby 107 (corner of Rothschild)* 03-5664277
Dizengoff 109 * 03-5221513

The biggest chain in Israel, notorious for opening branches
everywhere, pushing the cool specialist bookshops out of the way
and then selling predominantly best sellers and mass market
stuff. Unfortunately, as far as English and other foreign language
books, guides, maps, etc., they have the best choice. The Allenby
store in particular has a basement full of discount English books.
Apart from that they have branches all over the city and in every
shopping centre. Their biggest competitor is **Tzomet Sfarim**
who also has a good selection of English books for sale. You can
find their stores in Dizengoff Center (level 3), the Azrieli Center
and haTachana shopping area, among others.

Sipur Pashut
http://www.sipurpashut.com
Shabazi 36 * 03-5107040 * Sun – Thur 9:00 – 20:00, Fri 9:30 –
16:00

A gem of an independent bookstore hidden away in Neve
Tzedek's little streets. They carry a good selection of English titles
and you can also order books through them. There's a cozy
upstairs space for curling up with your books.

Hamigdalor (The lighthouse)
http://www.hamigdalor.co.il
Yehuda Halevi 51 * 03-6868225 * Sun – Thur 10:00-19:00, Fri
10:00-15:00

An inspiring independent bookstore specialising in books from
small, independent publishers from Israel and abroad. They also

do a good range of posters, games and apparel based on popular books / book characters and can help you track down rare books.

Dikler
Allenby 81 * 03-5660939 * Sun – Thurs 9:30 – 18:00, Fri 9:30 – 13:30

Sells new books in Spanish suitable for natives and students alike.

Landsberger
Ben Yehuda 116 * 03-5271395 * Sun – Thurs 11:00 – 19:00, Fri 10:00 – 13:00

Books in Hebrew, English and German. Supposedly you can order German books from Germany too.

For **used books**, try:

Book Junky
http://sites.google.com/site/bookjunkyisrael/
Dizengoff 167

Lots of cheap used books in English and other languages. You can also exchange your old books, CDs, etc. for store credit.

Pollack
King George 36 * 03-5288613

Hebrew and English used books, some rare.

Bibliophile
Corner of Allenby and Geula

Lots of used English books and magazines.

Halper's books
Allenby 87 * 03-6299710

Used books in various languages (that whole area of Allenby is full of new and used book stores in all kinds of languages).

Simaniya
HaCarmel 8 (bottom end of Carmel Market)

A curious little shop packed with cheap used books in Hebrew, English, French, German and Russian. Some good finds.

Shimon Rokah 26 (Neve Tzedek)

Free used books left out on shelves in the street as a gift to the community. Many are in English. Take as many as you want, leave some if you like and you can also leave a donation.

There's also a good used book store inside the Central Bus Station, level 3, store no. 3089. They carry used books in various languages including English and Russian.

For **Comic books** try:

Comics N Vegetables
King George 40 * 03-6204847 * Sun – Thurs 10:30 – 21:00, Fri 10:30 – 16:30

A funky, well stocked store selling both foreign and local comic books, toys, manga stuff, etc.

Comikaza
http://comikaza.co.il
Dizengoff Center, Building B, 2nd floor (Near Tzomet Sfarim bookshop) * 03-620-5684

Reopened as a physical store in Oct 2013 and is well stocked and popular. Also have an online store.

Art & Design

Bauhaus Center
http://www.bauhaus-center.com
Dizengoff 99 * 03-5220249 * info@bauhaus-center.com
Sun – Thurs 10:00 – 19:30, Fri 10:00 – 2:30, Sat 12:00 – 7:30

This place is where you should go if you're interested in Bauhaus or general cool design / art stuff. It's basically a gift shop, gallery and book shop where you can also join English speaking architecture tours (or buy maps / guides / books and do it without a tour). The place is geared for tourists (read: everything in the shop is expensive), but you can't fault their flawless knowledge of the city's buildings and their history.

Arta
http://www.arta-israel.co.il
King George 47 * 03 – 5289785
Nachlat Binyamin 83 * 03 – 5601926
Sun – Thurs 8:00 – 19:00, Fri 8:00 – 14:00

Two branches of a big chain selling a big selection of art & craft supplies, stationary, etc. Good if you're so inspired by Tel Aviv, you want to draw or make something.

Music

Haozen Hashlishit
http://www.third-ear.com (Hebrew only)
King George 48 * 03-6215223 * info@third-ear.com
Sun – Thurs 10:00 -23:30, Fri 10:00 – 18:00

Tel Aviv's best music store without a doubt - a big place selling new and used music, DVDs, games, magazines and concert tickets (well, those aren't used). The emphasis is on cool, alternative things and the staff are incredibly knowledgeable and helpful. This is also Tel Aviv's best DVD library with all kinds of cult movies and TV shows, anime, cool documentaries, sci-fi, horror music DVDs, etc. There is also a bar / performance space here, **Ozen Bar** (see Music section). I could rant and rave about this place all day, but it's better if you just go and check it out.

Hor beshachor
http://www.blackholerecords.net(Hebrew only)
Shlomo Hamelech 5 * 03-5285388
Mon – Fri 10:00 – 20:00, Fri 10:00 – 16:00

This store's been around for years and years and sells new and second hand CDs and DVDs. People in Tel Aviv have obscure, eclectic tastes, so you may well find some magical things here, although the prices aren't generally of bargain-bin variety.

UFO Music
Dizengoff Center, building B, Gate 6 * 03 – 5257666
Sun – Thurs 11:00 – 21:00, Fri 10:00 – 15:00

Specialise in rock and alternative music of various kinds and sell T-shirts, posters, piercing jewellery and tickets to gigs (including big name visiting rock/metal/alternative bands).

Metal Shop

http://www.metalshop.co.il * info@metalshop.co.il
Pinsker 27 * Sun – Thurs 10:00 – 22:00, Fri 10:00 – 16:00

The clue is in the name – this place is all about metal music in all its forms, from trash to glam and far far beyond. They sell CDs, posters, concert tickets, etc..

Misc

Achoti

Shlomo Hamelech 4 * 077-4011271
Sun – Thurs 10:00 – 20:00, Fri 10:00 – 14:00

The best place in town to buy meaningful gifts to take home - a fair trade gift store run by a co-operative of Jewish and Arab women. They sell speciality foods like olive oil, herbs, spices and conserves as well as beautiful handmade baskets, bags, pottery and toys. The money made helps empower local women.

Shoshana

Sheinkin 58 * 03-5609049, 052- 5605557
Daily apart from Sat at random hours. Call to confirm or to arrange specific times.

A quirky little store selling mostly vintage old stock toys and collectibles from Israel and beyond. You could easily spend an hour or more going through the stuff on sale and reliving childhood memories (yours or someone else's). The shop is run by a little old lady who's just as quirky as the stuff she sells.

Bara Herbs
http://www.bara.co.il
Dizengoff 132 (corner of Gordon) * 03-5240648 * Sun – Thurs 10:00 – 20:00, Friday till early afternoon.

A herbal medicine and natural cosmetics concept store offering potent herbal products to help with everything that ails you, as well as exciting lotions and potions of all kinds to make you beautiful.

Bait Banamal (Home in the Harbour)
http://www.comme-il-faut.com/house
Hangar 26, Tel Aviv Port * Sun-Thur, Sat 10:00-22:00, Fri 10:00-16:00

Upmarket, modern and a bit pretentious (as you'd expect in the port area) this self-proclaimed "department store" is a big, bright space designed by women for women. It's headed by the ladies who run fashion label Comme Il Faut and is certainly beautifully designed. There's an exhibition space with interesting shows, fair trade products (from the Achoti store, above) arty things, a restaurant, interesting cultural events on occasion and, of course, clothing and accessories both new and vintage.

Online Shopping

Not in Tel Aviv? You can still buy some stuff from independent Israeli designers, artists and makers.

General

http://market.marmelada.co.il – Sort of like the Israeli Etsy, this site is full of little independent virtual stores selling everything from art to design, fashion, furniture and anything else you can think of. The catch? It's Hebrew only. Google translate does a good job, though and the checkout is Paypal.

Art, design and related stuff

50*70 - http://5070.co.il
An online store selling prints by local artists, photographers and designers. Hebrew only for now, but Google Translate works.

Baalei Hamelaha - http://market.marmelada.co.il/hamelaha
Pretty prints in various styles, including a whole series of Tel Aviv themed posters. Hebrew only so use Google Translate.

Postdesigner - http://www.postdesigner.com
Tel Aviv based artist Gabby Nathan sells mindblowing paintings, prints and T-shirts.

Pilpeled - http://pilpeled.com
Somewhat twisted prints, T-shirts and other merch from this talented artist, responsible for the limited edition Israeli Absolut Vodka bottle design.

GhosTown Crew - http://ghostowncrew.com
These guys are actually from Haifa, but are so cool, I'm willing to ignore that and put them here anyway. If you like street art, then you will agree with me.

Red Elk - http://market.marmelada.co.il/redelk
http://www.etsy.com/shop/redelkshop (different products in the different stores)
Beautiful handmade toys and bags, as well as pretty and weird art prints.

Fashion and accessories

PetitMort - http://www.etsy.com/shop/PetiteMortShop
Unique jewllery made with metal crochet and semi-precious stones.

Jen Fashion- http://www.etsy.com/shop/jenfashion
Classy and elegant smart casual clothes for women

PlazmaLab
http://www.plazmalab.com

Funky T shirts and hoodies for men and women plus more club and streetwear and accessories.

Gelada Studio
https://www.facebook.com/geladastudio

Very hip T shirts for men and women.

FreeSpirit Design -
https://www.facebook.com/FreeSpirit.Design
Inspired by the Israel-Goa psy trance scene, these pretty party clothes are usually sold at festival and full moon parties around the world. Now you can get them online too.

7 Do Stuff

Hang out

The beach and the Tayelet

The beach occupies the entire western stretch of Tel Aviv. The Tayelet is the Hebrew name for the beach promenade. Most tourists head straight to the beach, or, rather, the beaches, as the seafront is divided into a whole load of different beaches with different vibes, cafés and visitors. Everyone in Tel Aviv has his or her favourite beach, so the best thing to do is take a walk and discover your own. Hilton beach (by the Hilton hotel) is the one favoured by the city's gay crowd. The Dolphinarium beach often has juggling and fire meet ups (see below), while Mezizim (Metsitsim or Metzitzim) Beach further north has Friday afternoon beach parties during the summer. The marina up near Ben Gurion Blvd. is nice for a wander and if you head north past Mezizim beach beyond the port an the Reading power station, you'll find a nice stretch of relatively empty beaches past the Yarkon river estuary with a path stretching practically all the way to Herzlia – great for cycling or hiking.

Alma Beach by the southern end of Charles Clore Park is probably the coolest beach (and the café by the same name serves amazing frozen arak slushies in the summer). Head even further south towards Jaffa past the Etzel museum for a more surreal cross-cultural beach experience, but not if you're afraid of dogs – owners are allowed to keep them off their leash here.

Hayarkon Park

Tel Aviv's main and biggest park stretches along both sides of the Yarkon river that separates Tel Aviv's Old North from the northern neighbourhoods. You could walk or cycle along the river all the way to the river's origin, well outside down (takes a few hours). The park is great for riverside picnics. BBQs are allowed to the East of the Ibn Gavirol bridge, but not on the Western side.

There is a big sports centre in the park, the Sportek (Sderot Rokach 42 * 03-6990307) with a climbing wall, a skate park and other sporting facilities (various ball game fields, tennis, etc.). You can rent rollerblades here, too. Further east past the Ayalon motorway, there is a big waterslide park (http://www.meymadion.co.il) and, across the road, the Luna Park – Tel Aviv's fairground / amusement park with rollercoasters, etc. (http://www.lunapark.co.il). If you carry on east along the southern bank towards Ramat Gan, things get even greener, with woods, an artificial lake and some interesting historic sites.

Other (much smaller) parks of note include **Gan Meir** (no real lawn, but it has a lovely pond and ping pong tables and is great for watching Tel Aviv's largest population of fruit bats) and the seaside parks **Charles Clore** (whose flat lawns are the favourite weekend BBQ spot for Jaffa residents) and **Gan Haatzmaut**, a pretty park that used to be a big gay cruising area but has been renewed and the council is now actively discouraging that (for better or for worse).

Tours, workshops, lectures

Alternative ways of Learning Hebrew

This is not an ulpan
notanulpan@gmail.com * http://goo.gl/YhXeI (Facebook group)

An alternative to your standard "ulpan" (Hebrew school) experience. Instead of learning Hebrew, students learn *in* Hebrew, critically debating and learning about issues that affect Israel and Israeli culture. There are classes suitable for beginners, intermediate and advance students. Among the topics are things like language and culture, Israeli feminism, militarism in Israeli culture and collective identity.

Streetwise Hebrew
http://www.streetwisehebrew.com

This guy offers fun local graffiti tours and Hebrew classes using street art and street sign typography. You can also learn lots of Hebrew slang!

Spaces and centres

Baalei Hamelaha
http://www.hamelaha.co.il
Y K Peretz 15 * 03-5370773 * office@hamelaha.co.il

A print studio and gallery that also holds courses, workshops and lectures on all aspects of traditional printmaking and related arts and crafts. You can also buy various printed items on site and via their online store.

Mazeh 9

https://www.facebook.com/mazeh9

Mazeh 9 * 03-525-7490 * mazehnine@gmail.com * Sun – Thur 9:00 – 22:00+

A place set up by the Tel Aviv municipality to serve as a hub for young people (up to 35). Sort of a free communal work / study space where you can hold meetings or rehearsals, use the Internet or attend various lectures, film screenings and events.

Hub Tel Aviv

http://www.the-hub.co.il * Derech Begin 55 (Maariv House) 7th floor * 03-6245410 * hub.tlv@gmail.com

The Tel Aviv branch of the Hub network of social enterprise centres. Apart from providing shared workspace, office space and studios for members (not cheap, but cheaper than renting a whole office and with a better atmosphere), they also have regular interesting workshops, lectures, film showings and other interesting events that are sometimes in English. You might need to email them for English listings.

For similar spaces for startups and entrepreneurs check out The **Library**'s website - http://www.thelibrary.co.il/foreign-visitors.html where there is also a list of additional workspaces.

Google Campus TLV

http://www.campustelaviv.com

If you're at all technically / Internetly minded, it's worth keeping an eye on the programme of (mostly) free events on Google's local learning campus. Interesting seminars, talks and conferences are common and some are held in English. You can also apply to hold your own related event here.

Tel Aviv Makers (TAMI)
http://telavivmakers.org

A Tel Aviv hacker space for meeting, talking and making. A good place to meet fellow makers and work on various projects.

Garage Geeks
http://www.garagegeeks.org

Another Hack space in the general Tel Aviv area - a non-profit group of cool geeks and tinkerers operating from a big industrial space in Holon (about 8km from South Tel Aviv). Check their website or sign up to their blog to get updates on their events. They have a monthly lecture series with some of the biggest international names in technology and computing. These are open to the public and happen at various venues in and around Tel Aviv. They also have more underground meet ups for networking, gaming and working on projects. You need to email them to get details of those, but places for new people are very limited.

Tours

CTLV
http://ctlv.org.il

Art tours and unusual urban tours, great for getting interesting insights about life in Tel Aviv not usually experienced by tourists. They hold regular tours to Tel Aviv's southern neighbourhoods – great if you want a soft introduction to the city's grittier sides.

Green Olive Tours (listed in the study tours section of the **Volunteering, Activism, Politics** chapter) have an interesting day / half day tour of Jaffa that's always held in English.

***

For official **English-languages guided walking tours of Tel Aviv** (history, architecture, etc.) You can try http://www.visit-tlv.com (the council's official tourism site). The Tel Aviv University one comes highly recommended as an alternative to the usual White City tour (if you've had your fill of Bauhaus). It's also worth checking http://www.batim-il.org if you're in town around May, for tours and events happening as part of the Tel Aviv open house weekend.

If you want to see some Bauhaus building without joining an actual tour, check out the **Bauhaus Center** in the art section of the **Buy Stuff** section.

***

Other workshops

City Tree
http://www.citytree.net
Bialik 25, Flat 7 (on the square, used to at 23) * 03-5254196 * tree@citytree.net

A lovely social enterprise encouraging urban sustainable living. It's run from a lived-in flat – a living example of how you can live ethically and eco-consciously even in a city. They offer all kinds of interesting workshops there and elsewhere, like compost making, nutrition, vegan cooking and chocolate / ice cream making, permaculture, etc. They often have an open house and "lunch break" sessions where you can eat a cheap vegan meal and learn

about eco living. Email to find out what's going on.
If you want to try your hand at community gardening, you could also try the community garden on HaRav Kuk St. (organised activities Mondays from 16:00 and Fridays from 14:00).

Sun-kissed Foods
http://inbariko.wix.com/sun-kissed-heb (Hebrew only)
0547275353 * inbariko@gmail.com

Want to learn how to make the perfect hummus? This lovely lady will teach you the secrets of tasty and healthy cooking, which also happens to be vegan / vegetarian – no preaching! She holds regular workshops in south Tel Aviv. Workshops include everything from preparing full vegan and raw meals to making hummus, vegan desserts, chocolate and more.

Kitchen Talks
https://www.facebook.com/ProjectKitchenTalks
project.kitchentalks@gmail.com

A unique and wonderful projects offering intimate cooking classes in small groups with chefs and cooks from the asylum seeker community. On the menu is African food from various countries, often with a vegetarian / vegan focus but also occasionally with meat and fish. There is a different class with a different chef every week, usually on Friday mornings or Saturdays. Languages spoken include English, French, Arabic, Hebrew and more.

Hastudia
http://hastudia.blogspot.co.il

A friendly art & crafts studio / hub in Jaffa hosting all kinds of cool workshops from DIY upcycling to woodworking, painting and more.

Yoga and meditation

Also, see **Studio Naim** in the Dance section for other good yoga classes.

Bikram Yoga
http://www.bikramyogaisrael.co.il
Karlibach (or Carlebach) 14 and Dizengoff Center, next to **Gymmi** (see below)* 03-6241807

English classes. The main Tel Aviv centre for this demanding yoga style practiced in a heated room. It's a bit too insane for me, but I have it on good authority that it's true to style and very much hardcore. They often have an introductory offer where you can do as many classes as you like over one week for only 100NIS. There are classes every day of the week and currently, 3 are taught in English.

Sivananda Yoga
http://sivananda.co.il(Hebrew Only)
Latris (or Letteris) 6 * 03-6961810 (you can call between 10:00 - 22:00)

The Tel Aviv branch of the big international Sivananda organisation, teaching classical yoga – no heated rooms, jumping about, etc. but more than your fair share of pre-action chanting and adopted Indian names. They have several classes a day (no classes on Saturdays, limited classes on Fridays) and their teachers are all good and very thorough. Classes are taught in Hebrew. Speak to them in advance if you need them to address you in English. They have a free class every Monday at 18:00.

Mishkan Hayoga
http://www.ashtanga-yoga-israel.com
Kompert 6 (first floor) * Carlibach 14 *
mishkan.hayoga@gmail.com

Tel Aviv's longest running Ashtanga centre run by a lovely couple.
The level of tuition is extremely high, but they predominantly
offer full courses nowadays, rather than drop in classes.
Occasionally there are interesting workshops, some with big
name international teachers.

Chandra Yoga
http://chandra-yoga.com
Ishtori Haparhi 4 * 03-5464045

They teach Ashtanga, Iyengar and Vinyasa yoga, as well as
Pilates for Yogis. There are also monthly Vipasana classes.

Yogini
http://yogini.co.il
Rothschild 4 * 054-7837529

Vijnana, Vinyasa, pregnancy & baby yoga plus some dance
classes. They also offer a 10NIS yoga class on Wednesdays, by
the same teacher who teaches the 10NIS classes at **Studio
Naim** (see Dance section)

Neve Tsedek Iyengar Yoga Center
http://www.yoga-center.co.il
Shlush 2 * 03-5163641 * yoga@yoga-center.co.il

Established for 15 years in scenic Neve Tsedek, this place teaches
the Iyengar form and is affiliated with the centre in Pune. Great if
you want a slower, more precise form of yoga.

Osho Israel
http://www.oshoisrael.co.il
Idelson 5, flat 1 * 052-8883040 * oshoisrael@gmail.com

Weekly Osho meditation classes that can be taught in English.
They also offer weekend workshops that are generally taught in
English as standard.

Exercise, swimming and pilates

Gymmi
Dizengoff Center, Building B on the roof (3-4 floor, take the glass
lift to the 4th floor, or the escalators to the 3rd floor) * 03 –
6204116, 03 – 6201130

Great location and the place is open 24/7 with a fully stocked
gym and a covered, heated swimming pool. A single visit
currently costs around 70NIS.

Gordon Pool
Eliezer Peri 14 (by the Tel Aviv marina, on the beach) * 03-
7623300

Tel Aviv's historic seaside swimming pool in its newest form
overlooks the pretty marina and the sea and now has a big gym
as well. The water in the pools (one Olympic and two for kids) is
"salty ground water", so pretty much like sea water minus Tel
Aviv's crazy currents.

Dror Raz Pilates
http://www.pilates.co.il/49316/About_Dror_Raz_Pilates *
pilatestlv@pilates.co.il * Yehieli 5 (Suzanne Dellal Centre) * 03 –
5108527

One of Tel Aviv's original Pilates places at a great location in
scenic Neve Tzedek. Mixed matwork / equipment classes in small
groups of up to 6 people. Not cheap, but the quality of tuition is
high. Contact them for free intro class.

Also see **Studio Naim** in the dance section for Pilates classes.

Tel Aviv University Sports Centre
http://www.sports-center.co.il
Haim Levanon 50 * 03-6408909

A big sports complex with several swimming pools (including an
Olympic swimming pool), a gym, tennis courts, etc. Single entry
tickets available and students get discounts.

Free Gyms
1. On the Tayelet, opposite Geula street
2. On the Tayelet, North-eastern end of Charles Clore Park
3. On the Tayelet, Gordon beach
4. Ganei Yehoshua, Yarkon Park (North bank) East of Netivei
Ayalon (the big motorway)

The city has set up some gym equipment at the beach and in the
Yarkon Park, so you can get a full body workout and even
combine it with some running or cycling. The machines are
simple but effective. On sunny weekends they are often crawling
with kids. Otherwise, they are usually not that busy. There are
more scattered around town.

Dancing

Dance Tel Aviv
http://www.dancetelaviv.co.il
Address: Dizengof 98 (4th floor) * Phone: 03-5220215

A popular dance studio offering classes in salsa, tango, ballroom and swing / lindy hop. They also have weekly practicas, milongas and swing dance parties that are very popular (no need to dress up, Tel Aviv's a fairly casual place). They do a good introductory offer where you can either get a free group class or pay 50 NIS and get a free group class, a half hour private lesson and free entry to one of their parties. Group classes are taught in Hebrew as standard but they'll happily incorporate English into the classes. No need to bring a partner.

Holy Lindyland
http://www.holylindyland.com

Fun and well-taught weekly lindy hop / swing / blues classes for all levels. Also parties, masterclasses and occasionally free classes at festivals and events.

Tango with Sylvia
http://www.tangoargentino.co.il

In my opinion, she's the best tango teacher in Tel Aviv, if not the whole of Israel. Also runs very popular milongas. Classes can be a bit cliquey.

Studio Naim
http://www.naim.org.il (Hebrew only)
Salame (or Shlomo) 46 * 03-5188998 * info@naim.org.il

A cool and friendly space offering various dance classes (classical and contemporary ballet, belly dancing, samba, african, Ethiopian, hip hop, etc.) plus contact improvisation, Capoeira, Pilates (now including a brand new equipment room with reformers) and yoga. English is well catered for and if you email, you can get their full class schedule. An intro class costs 30NIS (apart from African which costs a bit more). There is also a community yoga class on Mondays for only 10NIS. Their classes can get very busy so best to arrive early.

Sahara City
http://www.saharacity.co.il (Hebrew only) * Allenby 57 * 03-5252373 * saharac@netvision.net.il

A big, popular Egyptian style belly dancing school and costume design studio. They run classes throughout the week.

Suzanne Dellal Center
http://www.suzannedellal.org.il
Yehieli 5, Neve Tsedek * 03-5105656 * info@suzannedellal.org.il

Tel Aviv's best known dance center (watching, not dancing) is nonetheless as groundbreaking and breathtaking as can be. Some great stuff happens here from the worlds of dance, theatre and music.

Mayumana
http://www.mayumana.com

Israel's answer to Stomp – a high-energy, world class dance and rhythm company. Their space is based in Jaffa, just south of the old city.

Clipa Theatre
http://www.clipa.co.il

An exciting performance art space that hosts all kinds of interesting shows (Israeli and International), workshops and an annual festival with some really innovative performances (think Butoh, dance, physical theatre, ritual, puppets, etc.).

Juggling / circus / drumming/ Jamming

Gathering spaces

From spring onwards drummers and jugglers congregate on Friday afternoons at the **Dolphinarium beach** (north of the old Dolphinarium building, which is just north of Charles Clore Park) for an open jam. The same beach occasionally hosts Tel Aviv's fire juggling meets and Burner meets, usually on Saturdays. The area is soon to be redeveloped so time will tell if this habit stays.

During the sunny months, **Rothschild Blvd.** becomes busy with musicians and buskers on Friday afternoons. Walk up from Allenby St. towards Sheinkin to see stuff. There may be jams too.

Need supplies? There is a juggling supplies store at Eilat 46 (the street that ends up Derech Jaffa further East). It's open 8:00 – 17:00 Sun-Thurs and 10:00 – 14:00 on Fridays. There's a big music store in Dizengoff Centre, on the corner with Bar Giora street. For African drums, skins and straps, drumming lessons and drumming circles, try Tam Tam at www.tamtam.co.il (Hebrew only). You can email them at info@tamtam.co.il for more details.

Open stage / mic nights

For some reason, open mic nights are not that popular in Tel Aviv, nor do they generally happen in particularly hip places. For something that's at least not a giant tourist trap try:

Bar Giora (Bar Giora 4 * info@bargiyora.co.il * 03-6204880)

The open mic night is on Mondays. You need to sign up in advance. They often have local alternative rock bands perform.

For cooler open performance nights/festivals/events looking for people, check out my blog. I often list them there when they appear.

Water sports

SurfHouse
http://www.surfhouse.co.il
Gordon Beach * 03-5275927 * TLV.surfhouse@gmail.com

A surfing school for all kinds of surfing, including wind surfing, kite surfing, paddle boards and just plain surfing.

Octopus
http://www.scuba.co.il/eng
The Tel Aviv Marina (next to Gordon Beach) * 03-5271440 * telaviv@scuba.co.il

Established for nearly 30 years, this popular scuba diving school is a part of the SSI international network. Apart from running courses and organising dives in and around Tel Aviv, they can also organise dive trips to Eilat, Sinai and Jordan.

Elat Hayam
http://www.elat-hayam.co.il

A feminist yachting club in Jaffa, women owned and (mostly) women run. They offer short, romantic cruises in chartered yacht and also yachting / skipper courses.

Cinema

Apart from some releases of children's animated movies, all foreign films in Israel are subtitled and not dubbed. However, the subtitles are in Hebrew and sometimes also in Arabic or Russian so if the film isn't in a language you speak and you can't read Hebrew – you're screwed. Hebrew films are usually subtitled into English.

Israeli cinemas are generally cushy and pleasant and not overly expensive, unless the film in question is of the 3D variety.

Going to the cinema in Tel Aviv, you'll need to brace yourself for the annoying experience of having people use their mobile phones during the film. Usually you are spared this embarrassment in places like the Cinemateque or other showings of more high-brow films.

Gat

Ibn Gabirol 62 * 03 – 6967888

Blockbusters. Has 3D technology.

Lev

http://www.lev.co.il

Dizengoff Center, building A (top floor) * 03-6212222

Quality world cinema. Some blockbusters.

Rav Hen Dizengoff

Ben Ami 16 (Dizengoff Square) * 03-5282288

Blockbusters. 3D technology.

Cinemateque

http://www.cinema.co.il (Hebrew only)

Shprinzak 2 (corner of HaArbaa) * 03-6060800 (ticket sales), 03-6060819 (information)

Tel Aviv's repertory cinema. Remember that non-English films are not usually subtitled in English, so check before you get your tickets.

Midnight Cult

Israel has its fair share of homegrown psychedelic cult movies, the most famous of which are *Planet Blue* and the godawful *An American Hippie in Israel*. Look out for crazy midnight screenings on Friday nights (23:59) at the Cinemateque or pick up the DVDs at **HaOzen Hashlishit** (see the music section of the Buy Stuff chapter).

---

8 Art & Stuff

Tel Aviv has plenty of museums and galleries. If you wanted to, you could enjoy the cultural delights and free booze of gallery and show openings almost every single night. Here are a few galleries that tend to feature slightly more alternative things than the big museums and mainstream galleries. For regular listings of new openings and shows you can check out English language site OhSoArty (http://ohsoarty.com/). Local art magazine, http://erev-rav.com/ (Hebrew only, but Google Translate works well) is also very good. Most openings are on Thursday nights.

Spaces

P8
http://sites.google.com/site/p8artgallery/P8artgallery
Poriya 8, * 050-8616001 * Wed-Thur 16:00 – 19:00, Fri – Sat 11:00 – 14:00

An interesting, self-funded cooperative art space in that area between Jaffa and Tel Aviv.

CCA (Center for Contemporary Art)
http://cca.org.il
Kalisher 5 * 03- 5106111 * Mon – Thurs 14:00 – 19:00, Fri – Sat 10:00 – 14:00

A well-established art space showing groundbreaking time-based art from Israel and beyond. Apart from the exhibition space and events they also have a big video art archive.

Hahalalit

Hayarkon 70 * 03 – 5107071 * pigumim@hayarkon70.org * Hours vary. Try Sun – Thurs 11:00 – 19:00 and Fri 11:00 – 14:00 for shows, many events happen in the evening and on weekends.

A weird and super cool gallery in a flat on the top floor of an old building inhabited by young artists. Changing art shows and random events happen regularly from both alternative and well established artists.

Alfred Gallery

http://www.alfredgallery.com(Hebrew only)
Ben Atar 19 * alfred.hecht@gmail.com
Tues – Thurs 17:00 – 21:00, Fri 10:00 – 14:00, Sat 11:00 – 15:00

An independent gallery set up by a group of art graduates who got fed up of waiting for established galleries to accept their work. Changing exhibitions and events including paintings, photography, performance art and more.

Florentin 45

http://www.florentin45.com
Florentin 45 * 050-2763249
Mon-Thurs 18:00 – 21:00, Tues, Thurs-Sat 11:00 – 13:00

Cutting edge local underground and contemporary art. Some of Tel Aviv's best street artists exhibit here on occasion.

Sommer
http://www.sommergallery.com
Rothschild 13 * 03 – 5166400 * info@sommergallery.com * Mon – Thurs 10:00 – 18:00, Fri 10:00 – 14:00, Sat 11:00 – 13:00 (Sat closed in August)

A good sized space presenting well selected contemporary Israeli and foreign art, often with an underground edge.

Kayma
http://www.kayma.net
Ben Dosa 26, Jaffa * 03-6186144 * Tue – Thurs 11:00 – 17:00, Fri & Sat 11:00 – 14:00

An interesting art space in the trendy surroundings of the Jaffa flea market area.

Hahanut
http://www.facebook.com/hanut31
Haaliya 31 * hanut31@gmail.com

A small and unusual space in a converted shop with changing art shows and performance art events.

Indie
http://www.galleryindie.com
Yehuda Halevi 57 * Mon – Thur 11:00 – 14:00, 16:00 – 19:00, Fri – Sat 11:00 – 14:00

An interesting cooperative gallery space set up by a group of photographers.

Noga
http://nogagallery.com
Ahad Haam 60 * Mon – Thur 11:00 – 18:00, Fri - Sat 11:00-
14:00

Centrally located and with a good choice of established and
emerging local and international art shows.

Mika
http://mikagallery.co.il
Ben Yehuda 97 * Sun – Thur 10:00-19:00, Fri 10:00-14:00

A small gallery with interesting shows by emerging local and
international artists opening once a month.

Artport
http://www.artportlv.org
Ben Zvi 55 * artport@artportlv.org * 03-6073100

A centre for promoting young artists. Often has interesting
exhibitions and events on. Also offers residency opportunities.

The Israeli Center for Digital Art
http://www.digitalartlab.org.il
Address: HaAmoraim 4, Jessy Cohen neighbourhood, Holon * 03-
5568792 * info@digitalartlab.org.il
Tues – Wed 16:00 – 20:00, Thurs 10:00 – 14:00, Fri – Sat 10:00
– 15:00

Even though it's not actually in Tel Aviv but in Holon (a city just
south of Tel Aviv), this place is well worth visiting if you're into
video art, sound art and cutting edge digital arts. They also have
a very rich video art library where you could easily spend a day or
more watching things (call or email to arrange a visit). All
exhibitions are free. I recommend this place if you're a fan of the

genre, or interested in a particular exhibition they have on. Otherwise the journey is probably too much hassle to be worth it. A taxi is the best way to get there, though not cheap. Note that not all Tel Aviv taxi drivers know the place, so be sure to have the address on you. The above is the centre's new address, so some might know the old one (Yirmiyahu St.) Dan buses 72 & 129 and Egged buses 171 & 126 apparently stop nearby. You can get them from Allenby St. in Tel Aviv.

Other museums worth mentioning in Holon are the very small **Cartoon Museum** (http://www.cartoonmuseum.org.il) and the very impressive new **Design Museum** (http://www.dmh.org.il). Occasionally, there are some interesting multidisciplinary shows at the **Holon Institute of Technology** (http://hit.ac.il) as well.

Street Art

Tel Aviv has a prolific street art community and the city's streets are covered in brilliant artwork by local and visiting artists. Political works feature quite heavily, for obvious reasons, but there are also plenty of less loaded works. Many of the interesting pieces are in the Florentin area, predominantly in the narrow alleyways and back streets around Abarbanel Street (both sides) and the street itself. Take a walk around the **Comfort Club** (see clubbing section) and the nearby Florentin garden for some good works, old and new. There is also usually something good on Kfar Giladi St. just off the corner with Frenkel.

The nearby Neve Tsedek, also has a few very good works, check out the empty lots and the old rail tracks parallel to Derech Eilat.

Capzoola (Geula 42 * 0777059059 * Sun – Thurs 12:00 – 19:00, Fri 12:00 – 16:00) is the local street art store selling spray paint and offering an interesting (and tiny) gallery space and occasional events.

Street Art Links

A few popular artists whose works you'll see around town. Check out this Facebook page for more: http://on.fb.me/16mFIa0

KnowHope: http://www.thisislimbo.com/ (Know Hope on Facebook)

Foma: http://www.flickr.com/photos/fomafoma

Klone: http://www.flickr.com/people/klone

Shameless: http://www.flickr.com/photos/pnimibi

Zero Cents: http://www.flickr.com/photos/zerocents

Kufsonim: http://on.fb.me/10EsTzM

Inspire Collective: http://inspirecollective.blogspot.com

(see their site for details of their next group show in an abandoned building somewhere).

9 Party. Club. Gig.

Going out in Tel Aviv

As Friday is generally people's day off (along with Saturday) the weekend officially starts on Thursday night, which is when most of the big parties happen. Friday nights are also busy and those two nights are what the locals see as the "weekend" when it comes to partying all night. Saturday nights are usually quieter. That said, there's stuff going on every single night of the week in Tel Aviv, making it a clubber's heaven.

The people of Tel Aviv don't go out till late or they hang out in bars until the early hours and go clubbing afterwards. As a result, although parties officially start at midnight, 22:00 or even 21:00, nothing really gets going till after 1:00 or 2:00(AM). Gigs and concerts, of course, are different, as are gallery openings and launches.

Tel Aviv is small and there is always lots of stuff happening. The beauty of going out in Tel Aviv is giving in to the city's short attention span and sampling as many of its nightlife delights as possible. After all, everything is generally close together and the weather is usually nice enough for a casual wander.

Note: The BDS movement has been quite successful as of late in stopping many big name music acts from performing in Israel. You never know which international act is going to cancel last minute and the bigger they are the more likely they are to be under a lot of pressure not to perform. What I'm saying is don't get your hopes up too high if you've got a ticket for a non-local act.

Finding out what's happening

For big name local and international gigs and parties (as well as other types of big shows like circus, theatre etc.) you can check in with one of Tel Aviv's big ticket places:

Kastel Tickets
http://www.tkts.co.il(Hebrew only)
Ibn Gabirol 153 * 03-6045000
Sun – Thurs 9:00 – 19:00, Fri 9:00 – 1:30

Hadran
http://www.hadran.co.il(Hebrew only)
Ibn Gabirol 90 * 03 – 5215200

Mr Ticket
http://misterticket.co.il (Some English, accessed from top left of each event page)
03-5107070 * Phone support Sun – Thur 10:00 – 18:00 * Accept Paypal

Most of the cool clubby clothes stores and music stores in the shopping section carry flyers for smaller events and parties. Some will sell you tickets to gigs and parties too.

The streets and trendy eateries of Florentin are usually full of gig and party posters, most of which have English on them. You can also try individual artists' pages from the list at the end of this section. Some bars (Michatronix, Deli, Port Said, etc. see **Eat Out. Drink Out**) and the Abu Dubby hummus place (see **Buy Food. Eat Food)** also sell event tickets for some interesting things. Might be worth stopping by and asking what's available.

Listings Websites

The DIY Tel Aviv Blog: http://www.diytelavivguide.com/blog -
I update it with random cool stuff almost every day.

Tel Aviv City: http://www.telavivcity.com

A general Tel Aviv city guide, not particularly alternative, but Tel
Aviv is a small city and usually at least some underground events
are listed.

Isratrance: http://www.isratrance.com

Psychedelic trance is absolutely huge in Israel. This is a
psychedelic trance forum that lists various parties and club nights
around the country (and the world). The fact that it's a well
known site, monitored by the police, means that the parties listed
here are generally official ones in clubs or licensed outdoor
parties out of town. There's nothing too underground, unless
someone screws up and mentions something on the forums.

IrieLion: http://www.irielion.com

Israeli reggae listings, plus some world and ska. Reggae is also
huge in Israel.

Anova Music: http://www.anovamusic.com

The official page for this Israeli alternative music label, with gig
listings, plus the opportunity to listen to lots of cool local bands.

Midnight East

http://www.midnighteast.com

An English language culture blog / online magazine with a good eye for interesting stuff.

Facebook pages and websites for local underground party organisers

Some of these are very Hebrew-heavy, but if the event you're interested in it isn't listed in English, you can always post a comment and ask.

- **Submob Crew** – http://www.submobcrew.com – dubstep

- **Doof records** - hardcore psy-trance label that runs occasional outdoor parties and one famous underground festival. See Festivals section for more info

- **Moksha Project** - psy-trance parties in Tel Aviv plus outdoor parties elsewhere

- **TABAC** - the one that says "Tel Aviv bass consortium", underground dance parties

- **Infuse – Drum and bass nights, Israel**

- **T-Break** – breakbeat

- **Kidz Up Late** – dubstep and other bass music

- **Pacotek** - http://www.pacotek.com – techno / house

- **Global warming** (psychedelic trance parties, usually out of town) - http://www.globalwarming.co.il/events.asp

- **1984 -** http://www.facebook.com/#!/group.php?gid=185285232 40 – Dark 80s parties.

- **Swingotopia** – electro-swing retro parties

- **Roof Animals** - https://www.facebook.com/roof.animals - Tech / deep house parties, often on a roof.

- **Legotek** - https://www.facebook.com/lego.tek1 - tech house parties

- http://www.freetekno.co.il – free outdoor raves

- **Walk About Love** - http://walkaboutlove.org.il – outdoor Goa and psychedelic trance parties & festivals. Great vibe. Sometimes legal / authorised, sometimes not.

Clubs and venues

The Tel Aviv city council declared war on big clubs and some of the best ones have closed in the past few years. There are a few left, but the scene is mostly about small, intimate clubs and dance bars nowadays, plus one off underground parties in weird venues. Check out the bar section for dance bars and the Facebook pages above for tip offs about one off parties.

Dance Clubs

The Block

http://www.block-club.com/ (Hebrew only and crap)
Salame 157 (the New Central Bus Station Building) * 03-5378002
* office@block-club.com

The latest reincarnation of one of Tel Aviv's best underground clubs. It's big (for Tel Aviv) with several spaces, a state of the art soundsystem and an impressive line up of big name international DJs and acts - mostly electronic artists from techno to dubstep, plus some more experimental, cross-genre stuff. It upholds the smoking ban in the main dance spaces, though there is a smokers' lounge.

Comfort 13 (that's the address too, but spelled Kompert for some reason)

http://www.myspace.com/comfort13 * comfort13ta@gmail.com
Comfort 13, Comfort Echno and **Comfort Trance** on Facebook (different groups for different lines)

A big club for Tel Aviv (just over 400 capacity) down a dark alleyway. It has a decent sound system and if you stand in the right places you can actually breathe (through the smoke). It usually has band nights and gigs plus regular dance nights (mostly psychedelic trance and techno but also breaks, dubstep, reggae, etc.).

Gagarin

Gagarin Tel Aviv on Facebook * Salame 46 * 054-329-6596

As it's run and frequeted by Russian olim (immigrants), you'll hear much Russian spoken in this little club, tucked away at the back of a big courtyard. Door prices are cheap and nights vary from local metal, punk and indie rock gigs to trance, techno & bass music raves.

Haoman 17

http://www.myspace.com/haoman_17
Facebook group -
http://www.facebook.com/?ref=logo#!/group.php?v=wall&gid=6
693076145
Abarbanel 88 * 03 – 6813636

A biggish, expensive and very popular commercial club right next door to a big strip joint in the most industrial part of Florentin. They bring over some very big name dance DJs from abroad on a regular basis (Layo & Buschwacka, Derrick May, 2 Many DJs and loads more). Sadly, their sound system, while certainly loud enough, is also pretty shit and the place gets way way to crowded for comfort.

Bootleg

King George 48 * alon@bootlegclub.com

Used to be the Maxim club. A good club with two spaces, usually active on Thursdays / Fridays. The home of several 80s and dark 80s nostalgia nights, plus various electronic dance music nights.

Breakfast Club / Milk

Rothschild 6 * 054 - 7777997 * Almost every night, usually around 23:00 – very late

This popular place has a club-like space downstairs (the Breakfast Club) and a cool retro-ish dance bar upstairs (Milk). They have a good line up of parties, mostly in the house / tech house vein. Some gay / multisexual nights. Some events are free, others 30-50NIS.

Sublime
http://www.sublime.org.il (Hebrew only)
Salame 40 * 03-6298056, 03-5182528 *
sublime.bars@gmail.com

A big dance bar/ club / venue hosting predominantly local acts
and club nights of various styles (mostly of the rock / indie rock
variety but increasingly electronic music too).

Music Venues

Levontin 7
http://www.levontin7.com/(Hebrew only) * levontin7@gmail.com
Lavontin 7 (Google spelling)* 03- 5605084

A medium sized music venue run by musicians for musicians and
anyone who appreciates quality music of all genres. They have a
changing line up of gigs and club nights available on their
website. There's stuff going on just about every night with local
and / or international acts, including some wonderfully obscure
stuff. There is a separate bar area upstairs that's nice to sit in
and the venue itself is in the basement. They uphold the smoking
ban.

HaZimmer
http://zimmeramma.org (Hebrew only)
Hagdud Haivri 5 (corner of Chlenov, a door at the back of the
courtyard) * Most days from 21:00 – 00:00, Fridays 17:00 –
20:00

A music studio doubling as an underground performance /
exhibition space with a great atmosphere. It's in a slightly
unpleasant area (the fastest, easiest route is to walk up from
Allenby on Derech Menachem Begin and then turn onto Hagdud
Haivri). Events are always either free or very cheap and the

alcohol is super cheap. Some very cool and weird musical things happen here, as well as interesting art and performance art shows. Friday afternoons are generally free and there are usually random indie bands playing from around 17:00-20:00.

Koro
http://goo.gl/YykyW for Facebook page
Yizhak Sade 32 * xkoro32x@gmail.com

An alternative live music venue where the old Rogatka vegan punk bar used to be. It's a good place to catch all kinds of local alternative bands at cheap cheap prices. Lots of punk, hardcore and metal. Check their Facebook page for listings.

Haozen Bar
http://www.third-ear.com/ozenbar(Hebrew only)
King George 48 * 03-6215210 (Sun – Thurs 11:00 -15:00 for enquiries)

A neat space within the famous music store (see Haozen Hashlishit in the shopping section) playing host to various alternative gigs from rock to folk, electronica, jazz and the indefinably obscure. Sometimes there are electronic music nights there too.

Reality Rehab Center
(Reality Rehab Center on Facebook)
Beit Yosef 23 * 0524750755 \ 0547414760 *
bromofir@yahoo.com

A little performance / music / art space at Kerem haTeimanim that hosts intimate gigs by local underground bands. See Facebook group for listings.

Hangar 11

http://www.hangar11.co.il

Yordei Hasira 1 (Tel Aviv port) * 03 – 6020888

A big hangar turned into huge venue in Tel Aviv's moat commercial, overpriced clubbing area. Short of the stadium, this is one of the biggest venues in town if not the biggest, so sometimes you'll have no choice but to go here to see big name acts. It's not that bad, but it's not that great either. There are a few similar places in the port area.

Hateiva

http://www.hateiva.com (Hebrew only)* teiva@013.net

Sderot Yerushalayim (Jerusalem Blvd) 19, Jaffa (in "Hazerot Jaffa", parking level) *03-6822403

A good place to catch contemporary (classical) music concerts, plus occasional leftfield electronica, multimedia shows, performance art and genre-defying multidisciplinary performances. A bit chin-scratchy, but of very high standard. Unfortunately, their website doesn't currently seem to have any English on it, so you'll have to contact them to find out what's happening. This place is home to the 21st Century Ensemble (http://www.ensemble21.org.il) whose website does have an English section, so you can find out when they're on, at least.

Barby

http://www.barby.co.il (Hebrew only)

Kibbutz Galuyot 52 * 03 – 5188123

Probably the best acoustics and sound in Tel Aviv. A biggish, good-sized venue with big name local and, occasionally, international acts. Sometimes there are parties here as well.

Haezor

http://haezor.com

Harechev 13 * 054-4467240 * musicfromthezone@gmail.com *
Sun – Thur, Sat 21:00-4:00

A live music venue/lounge occupying the space that used to be
the Barzilay club. There are different shows by local musicians
every night from jazz to world music to rock, some free, some
not. They uphold the smoking ban.

Tmuna

http://www.tmu-na.org.il(Hebrew only)

Shuntsino 8 * 03 – 5629462

Fringe theatre, dance shows and occasional music gigs. Mostly
local acts of various alternative and cultural genres.

Zappa Club

http://www.zappa-club.co.il (Hebrew only)

Raul Valenberg 24 (Ziv Towers) * 03-7674646

Various music gigs by local and international music acts, mostly
jazz, world and what can only be described as eclectic. It's far
from the centre and the main tourist areas so you'll probably
need a taxi to get there.

Check out the talent

(Cool local bands and acts you might like)

Tiny Fingers: http://www.myspace.com/tifimusic/music

Electronic music meets rock – a really unique and promising
sound.

Taapet: http://taapet.com/

Great electronica from one of Israel's favourite underground electronic bands.

Umlala: http://www.myspace.com/umlalainuse

Clever and harmonic hipster-edged rock-pop.

Riff Cohen: http://www.facebook.com/riffcohen

French-Israeli pop with Middle Eastern touches.

Digital Me: http://www.myspace.com/digitalmekalzone

Funky, sampler-based electronica by one cool guy.

Oy Division: http://www.myspace.com/oydivision

Modern kleizmer (East European Jewish music) with a local cult following.

Electra: http://electramusic.com/

Alternative rock with 60s garage music influences.

System Ali: http://www.myspace.com/systemalijaffa

A cross cultural hip hop band from Jaffa, signing in Arabic, Hebrew, Russian and more.

Jack in the box: http://www.myspace.com/skipscapescoop

Lovely, melodic and weird pop music

Balkan Beat Box: http://www.balkanbeatbox.com

A hugely popular Israeli band that made it big across the sea as well. A funky blend of Balkan beats, rap, hip hop and electronica. Their stuff is heavily played all over town.

Hoodska: http://www.hoodska.com

A 7 piece traditional ska band.

Balkan Bamachsan:
http://www.myspace.com/balkanbamachsan

A 10 piece Middle Eastern / Balkan band with Jewish Klezmer and Arabic influences.

Izabo: http://www.izabomusic.com and
http://www.myspace.com/izaboband

Modern Arab funk with weird English lyrics. Played regularly all over town. Reunited to represent Israel in the Eurovision, but still alternative. Honest.

Marsh Dondurma: http://marshdondurma.com

A big street band with a big sound. If you like marching bands, you'll love these guys, though I am not sure they actually march.

Eatliz: http://www.eatliz.com

Hard, melodic alternative rock sung in English. You really want to see them live.

Naarot Reines (Reines Girls):
http://www.myspace.com/reinesgirls

Hebrew alternative rock

Terry Poison: http://www.terrypoison.com

Girly electro and Girlectronica

The Raw Men Empire:
http://www.myspace.com/therawmenempire

Surreal accoustic anti-folk niceness.

Lo Dubim: http://www.myspace.com/lodubim

Lefty Middle Eastern alternative rock

Hadugmaniot: http://www.myspace.com/hadugmaniot

Melodic alternative pop / rock

Midnight Peacocks:
http://www.myspace.com/midnightpeacocks

Middle Eastern alternative rock

The Ramirez Brothers: http://www.myspace.com/3ramirez

Israeli blues / rockabilly with a funky edge

The Apples: http://www.myspace.com/theapplesmusic

Amazingly tight funk with big sound and Middle Eastern touches.

Boom Pam: http://www.boompam.org

Mediterranean surf rock. Seriously.

Rutsi Buba

http://www.myspace.com/rutsibuba

Alternative rock / rockabilly. Not entirely unlike the Cramps.

Sun Tailor: http://www.suntailor.com

Beautiful and melodic rock/pop

The Angelcy: http://www.myspace.com/theangelcy

A biggish band with a really intelligent, quirky folky sound

Computer Camp: http://computercamp.bandcamp.com

Fun, danceable electronica.

3421: http://soundcloud.com/3421

A great dubstep outfit hailing from Haifa.

Mule Driver: http://soundcloud.com/muledriver

Awesome techno.

10 Volunteering, Activism, Politics

In this country being consciously a-political is the same as being political and is in itself taking a side – the government's side. In this guide, I chose to take a different side and invite you to see the reality of life in Israel, beyond both Hasbara and blind anti-Semitism. I know that as a tourist, you might not really care about the darker elements of life in Israel, which is fair enough, but if you're interested in finding out more about the conflict and other local problems or contribute your time (or money) to good causes while you're here (not just political ones) then this chapter is for you. This is my personal project so it has things that conform to my left wing, liberal politics and nothing to "balance" them out, as there's already plenty of that out there. Please feel free to skip the bits that don't sit well with your politics, though if you're trying to get a complete view of Israel and have only heard 100% pro-Israel stuff or 100% anti-Israel stuff so far, it might do you good to open your mind to other people's opinions.

Activism centres & locations

Yafa
Yehuda Margoza 33, Jaffa * Sun – Fri 8:00 – 23:00, Sat 10:00 - 23:00

A café in Jaffa that is also an active lending library and bookshop (Hebrew / Arabic / English) about the Middle East conflict. It acts as a meeting point for local lefty activists, both Jewish and Arab.

There are lectures and events and you can also take Arabic lessons upstairs. If you're not interested in politics, you'll still be able to enjoy the café, as tit's a relaxed and unusual place to just hang out.

Zochrot
http://www.nakbainhebrew.org
Ibn Gabirol 61, flat 2 * zochrot@netvision.net.il * 03-695 3155

This Israeli organisation aims to raise awareness of the Nakbah – the mass displacement of Palestinians during the 1948 Independence War. Much of today's Tel Aviv is built on the ruins of Palestinian villages. In fact, much of Israel is. These people didn't leave willingly and acknowledging what happened is the first step towards eventual reconciliation. Zochrot have a learning centre / exhibition space where you can learn more about this issue. It's open Mon and Thurs 12:00 – 17:00 or contact them to arrange a visit another time. They also run occasional study tours in Tel Aviv and beyond.

***

For an exciting activism centre out of Tel Aviv, contact EcoMe.Centre@gmail.com. It's an interesting workshop space near Jericho/the dead sea, accessible by both Israelis and Palestinians. They hold all kinds of exciting joint workshops from permaculture to conflict resolution. Do not confuse this with ecome.co.il which is something entirely unrelated.

Volunteering, internships, opportunities

General Humanitarian Causes

New Israel Fund
http://www.nif.org

A funding organisation fighting for social change in Israel and funding many grassroots organisations, not all political. Many of the organisations listed in this guide use the NIF to receive donations from abroad. The NIF offers 10 month fellowships in Israeli NGOs for post-college Jewish young adults and runs alternative organised trips to Israel from abroad. These are meant for both Jews and non-Jews to meet local likeminded activists and thinkers and learn more about Israeli society and the conflict. Unfortunately, they're not free (nor cheap), but are apparently amazing.

The Rosa Luxemburg Foundation
http://www.rosalux.co.il

The Israeli branch of this German organisation is in Tel Aviv and works with local charities and NGOs in the fields of: civic education and culture, higher education and research, communal activities, strengthening civil society and democratic participation, human and civil rights and protection of the environment. They take on English speaking interns for periods of at least 2 months.

Brit Olam
http://www.britolam.org

A Jewish volunteer organisation that's active in Israel and throughout the world. Some volunteering opportunities available in Israel / Tel Aviv, working with various disadvantaged local populations.

Tikkun Olam
http://tikkunolamisrael.org

A Jewish organisation that has various 5-10 month volunteering programmes in Tel Aviv for people aged 22-28. They involve working with refugees or new immigrants or fostering Jewish – Arab friendship. Accommodation and all kinds of fun extras are provided but you have to pay to join. Scholarships and grants are available that reduce the cost quite significantly, making it very reasonable.

Ruach Tova
http://www.ruachtova.org

An organisation that matches local NGOs with people interested in volunteering in Israel based on abilities and interests. They're very good at working with international volunteers.

SOS Violence
http://soscenter.org.il/eng

Targeting violence in Israeli schools as a way of creating deep social change in Israeli society. They offer plenty of friendly volunteering opportunities, both short and long term. English and other foreign language speakers welcome and they try to always give people interesting stuff to do.

Health

The refugee clinic

Hatachana Hamerkazit Hachadasha (new central bus station)
level 5, shop 5721 * Sun – Thur 16:00 – 20:00 *
orelbenari@gmail.com

This 100% volunteer-run clinic desperately needs help from
medics, carers and nurses (qualified or students) but also anyone
else who can be there to listen and help out. It's insanely busy,
so your emails may not always be answered quickly. Maybe try
visiting, but be aware the volunteers may be very busy and
stressed, so don't take it personally if they act it.

Physicians for Human Rights

http://www.phr.org.il

A brilliant organisation doing above and beyond for all of Israel's
disadvantaged populations – from operating field hospitals in
Gaza during the siege to giving much needed medical assistance
to Sudanese refugees and poor children in Israel. They take on
volunteers who don't speak Hebrew for various roles but unless
you have an Israeli doctor's license you won't be able to treat
patients.

Feminist/ women

Achoti

http://www.achoti.org.il
Matalon 70 * 03- 6870545

A feminist organisation helping disadvantaged women. Apart from
providing legal help and other types of support in their centre,
they also have a gallery space and occasional interesting events.

They are always looking for volunteers, though I'm not sure whether they have much use for non-Hebrew speakers. Also check out the **Achoti shop** in the Buy Stuff section, if you want to help the cause by buying cool stuff.

Sindyanna of Galilee
http://sindyanna.com/

A women-led organisation working to empower Israel-Arab/Palestinian women by producing fair trade products. They accept volunteers to help with things like olive picking, and you can also volunteer to teach workshops and classes to the women in their Galilee centre. They hold their own workshops where you can learn things like basket weaving and other traditional crafts. If you can't make it to the Galilee, you can buy their products from their Tel Aviv offices.

Kuchinate
http://www.kuchinate.com * kuchinate@gmail.com
Har Tsiyon 104, first floor * 054-9765667 (Diddy) / 052-7863483 (Natasha)

An African women refugee collective making and selling beautiful knitted baskets from recycled materials. Their studio is open every Sunday (call or email in advance if you want to go) and you can meet the ladies and buy their crafts. Volunteering opportunities are also available (email for details).

LGBT

Beit Dror
http://bethdror.org
Bustanai 13 (Neve Tzedek) * 03-5164621

A temporary shelter for LGBT teenagers in need of a place to stay after being kicked out of their homes because of their sexual orientation. They always need donations (money, food, goods) and volunteers to help out with everything from cooking to teaching workshops. May have some stuff non-Hebrew speakers can do.

Refugees & migrant workers

Foreign Workers Hotline
http://www.hotline.org.il

Providing much needed help to Israel's persecuted illegal alien and migrant worker population. They are always looking for donations and often for volunteers, especially those who speak both Hebrew and a foreign language.

Assaf
http://www.assaf.org.il

A very active and innovative organisation helping asylum seekers and refugees. Often have interesting volunteering opportunities.

ADRC
http://ardc-israel.org

Supporting African refugees in Israel. They are always looking for volunteers and much of their important and interesting work can be done by non-Hebrew speakers – volunteering in a woman's shelter, teaching English, interviewing refugees, helping out with events and more.

The Garden Library
http://www.thegardenlibrary.org/
http://bit.ly/H78U7O (Hebrew only, but more info)

A thing of beauty – a real lending library for refugees, foreign workers and their children in the middle of Levinsky Park, where many of them converge. They mostly need donations (of money and books in obscure languages), but also for volunteers to run workshops and activities for children and adults, as well as help run the library (translation from obscure languages, scanning, cataloguing, PHP/SQL programming and more). Email gardenlib@googlegroups.com or Eyal.feder@gmail.com for more details or visit the library (it's open Friday, Saturday and Sunday afternoons).

Political activism & study tours

While some activities listed here are held in English, many more are held in Hebrew. It might be worth going anyway if you have no other option, as Israelis speak good English and are usually keen to help out a foreigner. You don't have to be a diehard lefty to join most of the activities listed here. Being curious and having an open mind is enough.

Note that some demos and tours to the occupied territories can get you on the government's blacklist. If you're considering joining a tour or an activity in East Jerusalem or the other occupied territories, it won't hurt to ask the organisers whether the tours are OKed with the authorities and whether they know of anyone who's gotten into trouble following such an activity. This is especially true if the organisation or activity you are participating in has anything to do with the BDS (the call to boycott Israel). You can then make your own calculated risk assessment and decide on whether to go.

Ir Amim
http://www.ir-amim.org.il

This organisation runs weekly study tours of East Jerusalem so you can learn about the historical background and current socio-political situation in the city. These include a visit to sections of the separation wall. One tour a month is in English. The rest are in Hebrew.

Sheikh Jarrah Solidarity
http://www.en.justjlm.org/

Organise informative grassroots tours of East Jerusalem to educate about the problems faced by Palestinian neighbourhoods overtaken by Jewish settlers. Also demos and Israeli-Palestinian social activities.

Shovrim Shtika (breaking the silence)
http://www.shovrimshtika.org

This organisation was formed by ex soldiers to collect and document testimonials by former and current soldiers serving in the occupied territories and in Gaza. They run monthly tours (English and Hebrew) of Hebron and surrounding areas, where you can learn about the conflict, visit local Palestinian families and also see with your own eyes how badly the Palestinians are treated by local Jewish settlers. The tours actually leave from Jerusalem and very early in the morning so you'll need to either stay overnight in Jerusalem or get up very very early. You may be able to lift share if anyone else is coming from Tel Aviv. The tours are generally safe but pretty unpleasant. Sadly, they often get cancelled last minute by the army, as this is a sensitive area. For a good intro to the tours, you can watch the recent Louis Theroux Ultra Zionists documentary (try here: http://www.atheistmedia.com/2011/02/louis-theroux-ultra-zionists.html)

Anarchists Against the Wall
http://www.awalls.org

This direct action group is one of the spearheads of the Israeli left wing resistance movement and possibly the most hated by the government. They organise and participate in weekly demonstrations every Friday against the occupation and the separation wall anywhere that's currently controversial. Rides usually leave from Tel Aviv. Note that these are very hardcore, emotionally charged demonstrations and the army has been using a lot of tear gas and worse. Although supposedly non-violent demonstrations, violence always breaks out, usually, but not always, because of the army. Foreign demonstrators are often arrested and deported and some have even been hurt (or killed). Get as much info as you can before going to any of these. Be prepared.

Machsom Watch
http://www.machsomwatch.org

An organisation of Israeli women who monitor and document what's going on in the many checkpoints in and around the occupied territories. Both men and women can join their vigils and witness the daily reality of apartheid living. Vigils and tours are OKed with the army and are safe, although not pleasant.

The Israeli Committee Against House Demolitions
http://www.icahd.org

Organise very interesting and detailed day tours of East Jerusalem, as well as less frequent 10 day in-depth tours of Israel and the West bank for foreign nationals wishing to learn about the conflict firsthand.

The Palestinian Solidarity Project
http://palestinesolidarityproject.org

As far as I know, these are not connected to the ISM. They organise study tours of the agricultural Palestinian villages around Jerusalem to teach about daily life under the occupation and of Palestinian non-violent resistance.

Green Olive Tours
http://www.toursinenglish.com/

A neat Israeli-Palestinian social enterprise offering both day trips and longer tours in Israel and the occupied territories. They also have an interesting Jaffa walking tour. On out of town tours you can stay with Palestinian or Bedouim families, meet both settlers and Palestinians in the territories and get a different and interesting perspective about life in Israel.

Hanthala Hostel
http://www.hanthalahostel.com/tours

A Palestinian hostel in the old city of Hebron that offers free tours of the city to learn about issues to do with the occupation as experienced by Palestinians in Hebron.

Jerusalem Reality Tours
http://www.jerusalemrealitytours.com/

See life in Jerusalem and the issues faced by its different and diverse populations through the eyes of an Israeli peace activist.

Birthright Unplugged
http://www.birthrightunplugged.org

They organise radical study tours of the West bank for foreign nationals. Their aim is to counteract the Zionist Birthright tours' point of view by showing the complete opposite view. The tours seem to be quite hard hitting.

Sulha
http://www.sulha.com

They hold powerful monthly "tribal fire" meetings between Israelis and Palestinians. Mostly need donations but can also organise interesting tours and events for groups.

More peace organisations offering opportunities

Taayush
http://www.taayush.org

An Arab and Jewish partnership against the occupation. They organise occasional events and actions.

Coalition of women for peace
http://www.coalitionofwomen.org

A very active feminist peace organisation doing really good work. Very actively involved in most peace and anti-occupation demos. They occasionally organize interesting events and lectures.

Peace Now
http://www.peacenow.org.il

A long-running Israeli self proclaimed pro-peace Zionist organisation. You'll see them in most demos. Occasionally they organise interesting tours and events.

Combatants for Peace
http://www.combatantsforpeace.org

Former soldiers and Palestinian militants working together for peace. They occasionally organise interesting events and actions.

New Profile
http://www.newprofile.org

Helping Israeli conscientious objectors. You can help by sending letters of support to those imprisoned, contacting Israeli authorities and spreading the message about the struggle against the military state.

B'tselem
http://www.btselem.org

The Israeli information centre for human rights in the occupied territories. They do amazing work documenting and fighting violations on both sides. Interesting (though depressing) reports available on their site.

Rabbis for Human Rights
http://www.rhr.org.il

These guys are relentless in pursuing justice and supporting the disadvantaged. They organise interesting events and offer plenty of opportunities to help Palestinians within the framework of enlightened Judaism.

Yesh Din
http://www.yesh-din.org

Set up to oppose human rights violations against Palestinians by providing free legal help. Always looking for donations and may have limited volunteering opportunities for non-Hebrew speakers.

Halonot (Windows)
http://www.win-peace.org

A Palestinian and Jewish friendship organisation that operates youth activity centres, among other projects. They are Tel Aviv based and always looking for volunteers. They also organize occasional English language lectures and Arabic courses.

Animals, farming, environment

Anonymous
http://www.anonymous.org.il

The Israeli animal rights organisation. Take on volunteers and possibly have stuff that can be done by people who don't speak Hebrew.

Ginger / Zangvil

http://ginger.org.il (Hebrew only)

Balfur 8, Jerusalem * 02-5665737 * veginger@gmail.com

A vegetarian / vegan community centre in Jerusalem that also runs an organic co-op, a shop, workshops and a weekly communal meal (Thursdays from 19:00). They're looking for volunteers to help cook and serve the meal and it's OK if you don't know how to cook.

Wwoof Israel

http://www.wwoof.org.il/

The Israeli branch of the international network. If you sign up for annual membership with them (160NIS) you get access to a list of organic farms in Israel looking for volunteers in return for room and board. A few hours of work a day, 5 days a week will get you simple accommodation (for example, a caravan), plus food and a great experience, though not a volunteer visa.

The Arava institute

http://www.arava.org/

They have an interesting environmental studies programme and accept students and interns for things like their summer school.

Bustan

http://www.bustan.org

An Israeli organisation working with the Bedouim in the Negev desert. They have an interesting permaculture, Arabic & Middle Eastern studies programme you can join, plus tours and various other projects.

Go Eco
http://www.goeco.org/israel

They have all kinds of short, medium and long term volunteering opportunities in Israel – lots of interesting eco stuff, plus humanitarian things. They charge money for volunteering with them.

Volunteering on a kibbutz
http://www.kibbutz.org.il/volunteers/

It's not quite as in demand as it once was, plus the kibbutz movement is hardly the idealistic communist/socialist organisation it once was (more like ultra capitalist), but if you want to do hard physical labour for an Israeli kibbutz in return for room & board, you can still do it. Just. You'll need to register in advance while still in your own country and come here on a specific visa or leave the country and wait for a decision outside if you came in on a tourist visa. They apparently prefer Jews, Anglo-saxons and Europeans.

More Information

Some places online where you can get more info, find out about the news in Israel and get some alternative political commentary.

PAVI
http://www.israelvolunteering.org

A great source of information about activism and volunteering opportunities in Israel (not just political stuff but also social work, etc.), as well as info about alternative tourism and related local events.

Haaretz (in English)
http://www.haaretz.com

Israel's only broadsheet has an online English version. It's the most left leaning of all the major local papers and the best you can do in terms of decent Israeli news in English.

Indymedia Israel
http://indymedia.org.il

Providing alternative, independent news in Israel as part of the Independent Media Center network of sites. Plenty of English news, though some in Hebrew.

Who Profits
http://whoprofits.org

Israel has now passed the anti-boycott law, meaning that anything deemed to encourage people to not buy "Israeli products" (including products that come from the occupied territories) is an offence in the state of Israel. The above website, therefore, is here for novelty value only. It tells you which companies are making money from the occupation. What you do with that information is up to you.

972 Magazine
http://972mag.com

Independent, left wing political commentary and news from some of the most interesting voices in Israel. It's a good introduction to the so called "radical" Israeli left (or what's left of it).

Israel Social TV
http://tv.social.org.il

An alternative source for activism related news content. There are a lot of pieces in English.

TLV1
http://www.tlv1.fm

An English language online radio station broadcasting from Tel Aviv. They have some political talk shows that aim to be well balanced and informative.

11 Out of town festivals

Desert Ashram
http://www.desertashram.co.il

A few big festivals a year hosted by this Osho / Tantra community in the desert. They also offer regular workshops, work-meditation programmes, camping and B&B accomodation. Their festivals are generally 3 days long or longer and include reggae, world music, psychedelic trance, workshops, chai shops, psychedelic art and activities for children. The Intergalactic Raves happen around NYE and Purim, while the Zorba HaBuddha festival happens around Passover.

Doof Festival
(not mentioned on the label's website. Check the Doof Records Facebook page) * During Passover

A small festival for lovers of hard, high BPM psy-trance. There's an alternative stage playing other electronica in the day, but the majority of the music is of the above genre. Lovely location by water.

Boombanela
http://www.boombamela.co.il
(Usually during Passover)

A big, well-established, shanti themed gathering with live music, reggae, art, psychedelic trance and culture, spiritualism, workshops, etc..

Indigo Festival
http://www.indigofestival.co.il/

An electronic music festival that happens in June. Usually has a very good line up and a fun location.

Psilosiva
http://www.psilosiva.com

Hold big nature parties and the occasional festival. Psychedelic trance (including old school), chill out and more.

Sunbeat Festival
http://www.SunbeatFestival.com (seems to go to a Facebook page)

A 3 part festival (one each month in the summer months) of various kinds of global beats and world music.

Menashe Forests Festival
http://www.festivalyearotmenashe.com (Hebrew only)
Dates vary, either during Passover or in May

A friendly 3 day festival showcasing the best in local alternative rock, pop, dub and groove. There are also all kinds of art things, performance stuff and fun workshops, including some activities for kids.

InDNegev
http://indnegev.co.il/ (Hebrew only)
October

All kinds of local indie acts...in the Negev desert. Get it? Rock, indie pop, electronic dance music and chin-scratching electronica, you name it. There's something for everyone and the vibe is awesome.

Hanger Adama
(http://www.adama.org.il)

A unique dance / aerial dance school based in an old hanger in the old industrial area of the sleepy desert town of Mitzpe Ramon. Check it out for unusual music, dance and art events plus festivals, workshops and courses. Usually there's big(ish) stuff going on during Hannukah, New Year's Eve, Passover and other holidays. They also offer rustic B&B accommodation that can be combined with taking classes at the school.

Eilat International Bellydance Festival
http://www.eilatfestival.com
January or February

Israel's "Kosher Vegas" plays host to this brilliant festival celebrating bellydancing and Middle Eastern dance. Three days of workshops from some of the best local and international teachers plus haflas, performances and a bazaar. You can fly to Eilat from Tel Aviv relatively cheaply (takes about half an hour), or take a direct bus (a scenic 5 hour journey through the desert).

Out of town parties

These happen regularly, especially in the warmer months. Usually the music is psy-trance and often of the very hard, fast sort rather than the funkier melodic kind. The parties vary from one promoter to another, but in general the energy is good and the people friendly. Some of the locations are really very lovely with many parties happening in the desert. There's usually a single sound system playing through the night and maybe some stalls selling basic food and drink.

The legal or semi legal parties are often discussed on the Isratrance forum (see music listings section), but for the true underground parties you'll need to check the Facebook groups mentioned in the **Party. Club. Gig section**. You could also get your info from cool trancy people. Try going to something like Moksha in the big city (check the Moksha project Facebook group for info about these when they happen) and asking around there, or hang around places like Bazilikum Pizza in Florentin (see Buy good. Get food section) or anywhere else where you hear trance music playing or obvious India drop outs hang out.

Bigger events with big name acts may sell tickets via **Haozen Hashlishit** (Buy stuff section) **or Abu Dubby Hummus** (Buy food. Eat food section), otherwise it's a matter of getting tickets off some dude whose number was on the Facebook page.

You'll usually need your own means of transport to get to out of town "mesibot teva" (nature parties), although some of the bigger ones offer ride sharing forums. Try also posting on the event page. Some info lines (for the location of the party) are in Hebrew only, so you may need to get a local to help. Just be sure to NOT ask a friendly cop for help. ☺

Random Index

A

Acupuncture, 166
Airport security, 15
Arak, 42, 43, 45, 125, 176

B

Belly dancing, 155, 188
Busking, 189

C

Cake, 11, 22, 92, 93, 95, 103, 147
Cocktails, 106, 107, 119

D

Dance bar, 103, 125, 126, 203,
 205, 206

E

Electronica, 107, 127, 207, 208,
 210, 211, 213, 232, 233

F

Falafel, 81, 84, 85, 86, 120

G

Gay and lesbian, 38, 39, 40, 105,
 131, 132, 142, 154, 176, 177
Geek stuff, 180
Goth, 154

H

Hair, 164
Hip hop, 188, 210, 211
Hipster, 127, 154, 162, 210
Hummus, 18, 81, 82, 84, 85, 86,
 91, 95, 110, 120, 122

K

Khat (gat), 45

M

Morning after pill, 40, 41

P

Performance, 126, 154, 171, 189,
 190, 194, 195, 206, 207, 208,
 233
Pick up bar, 135
Pizza, 11, 17, 22, 81, 88, 89, 100,
 103, 113, 114
Psychedelic, 44, 192, 201, 203,
 204, 232, 233

R

Reggae, 85, 201, 204, 232
Rock, 107, 114, 127, 132, 135,
  139, 155, 171, 190, 206, 207,
  209, 210, 211, 212, 213, 233

S

Sandwiches, 93, 128, 142
Sexual health, 41
Shakshuka, 82, 83, 85, 91, 94, 111,
  145

T

Tattoos, 165

Taybe beer, 98, 99, 131
Techno, 202, 204, 213
Trance, 201, 202, 203, 204, 232,
  233, 234, 235

V

Vegan, 81, 82, 90, 100, 103, 108,
  115, 118, 119, 120, 121, 122,
  124, 136, 158, 163, 181, 228
Vegetarian, 103, 113, 115, 116,
  119, 120, 121, 124, 136, 228

W

Weed, 44, 45

NOTES

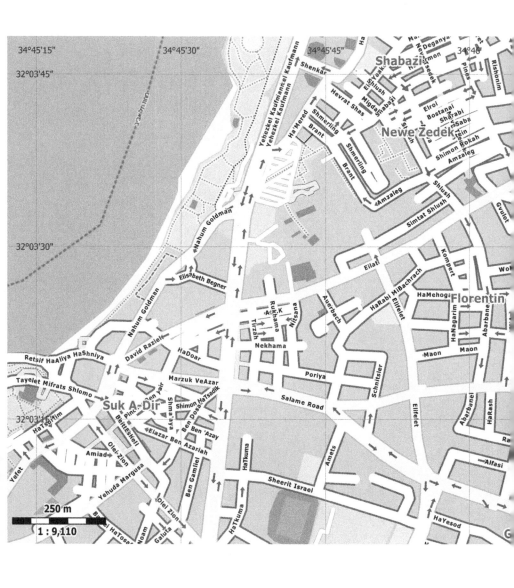

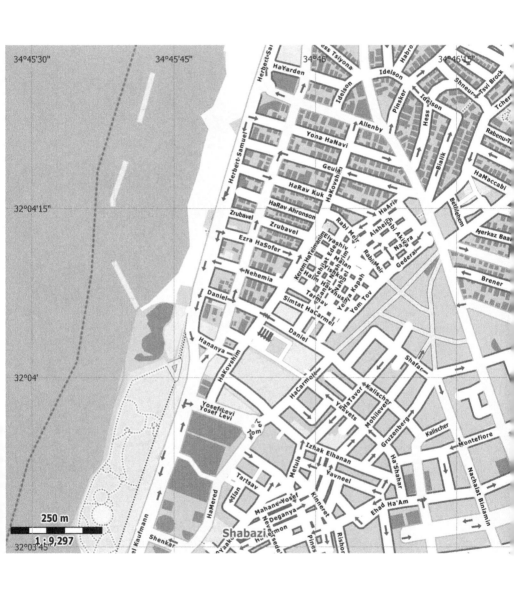

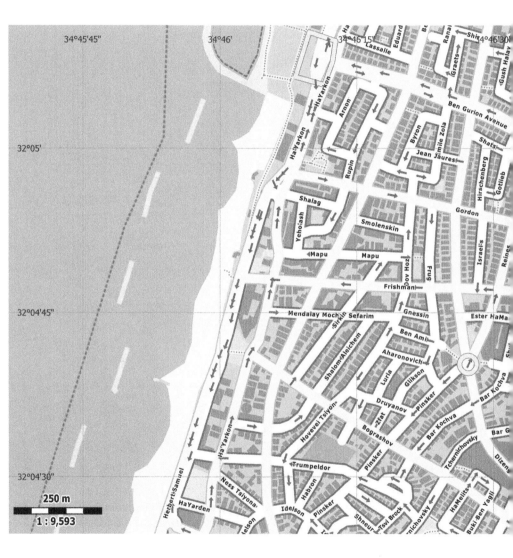

34°47′   34°47′15″   34°47′30″   34°47′

Israel Trail

Gviroi

Beili

Bar-Yehuda

Bney Dan

Bney Dan

HaRav Amiel

Nissenboim

HaRav Zirison

Namir Road

HaZohar

HaRav

Shlomtsion HaMalka

Matityahu

Stricker

Bublick

Pineles

Ve'idat-Katovich

HaRav Friedman

HaZohar

Ha'Tirsi

Agripas

Yehuda Ha'Maccabi

Alexander Yanai

Brandeis

Stricker

Dr. B. Borenheimer

Sderot Smuts

Rav Tza'ir

Weizmann

Bnei Moshe

Antigonus

Louis Marshall

Louis Marshall

Miriam-HaHashmonait

De Haas

Stricker

Namir Road

Tenura

HaBashan

Pinkas

Pinkas

Jericho

Belkind

Ahavat Zion

Prof Schorr

Lipski

Hankin

Arie Akiva

Namir Road

Har Nevo

Mossinsohn

Epstein

Moser

Kohnstamm

Danin

Wissotsky

Ibn Gvirol

David Yellin

Biltmore

Moshe Sharet

Smilanski

Joshua Bin-Nun

Remez

Jabotinsky

Moshe Sharet

Azarya

Klonimus

Immanuel Ha'Romi

Ben Saruq

Ben-Shaprut

He Be'Iyar

Gloskin

Yehuda Gur

Ibn Gvirol

Ben Saruq

Hadera

Jabotinsky

Jabotinsky

Arlosoroff

Harizi

Lightning Source UK Ltd.
Milton Keynes UK
UKOW07f1107190115

244716UK00001B/191/P